Copyright © 2015 DJ Ron. Coloring Book For Adults

All Rights Reserved Worldwide

CRAZY CONES

&

THE TOTALLY MAD HOUSE

COLORING BOOK

CRAZY CONES

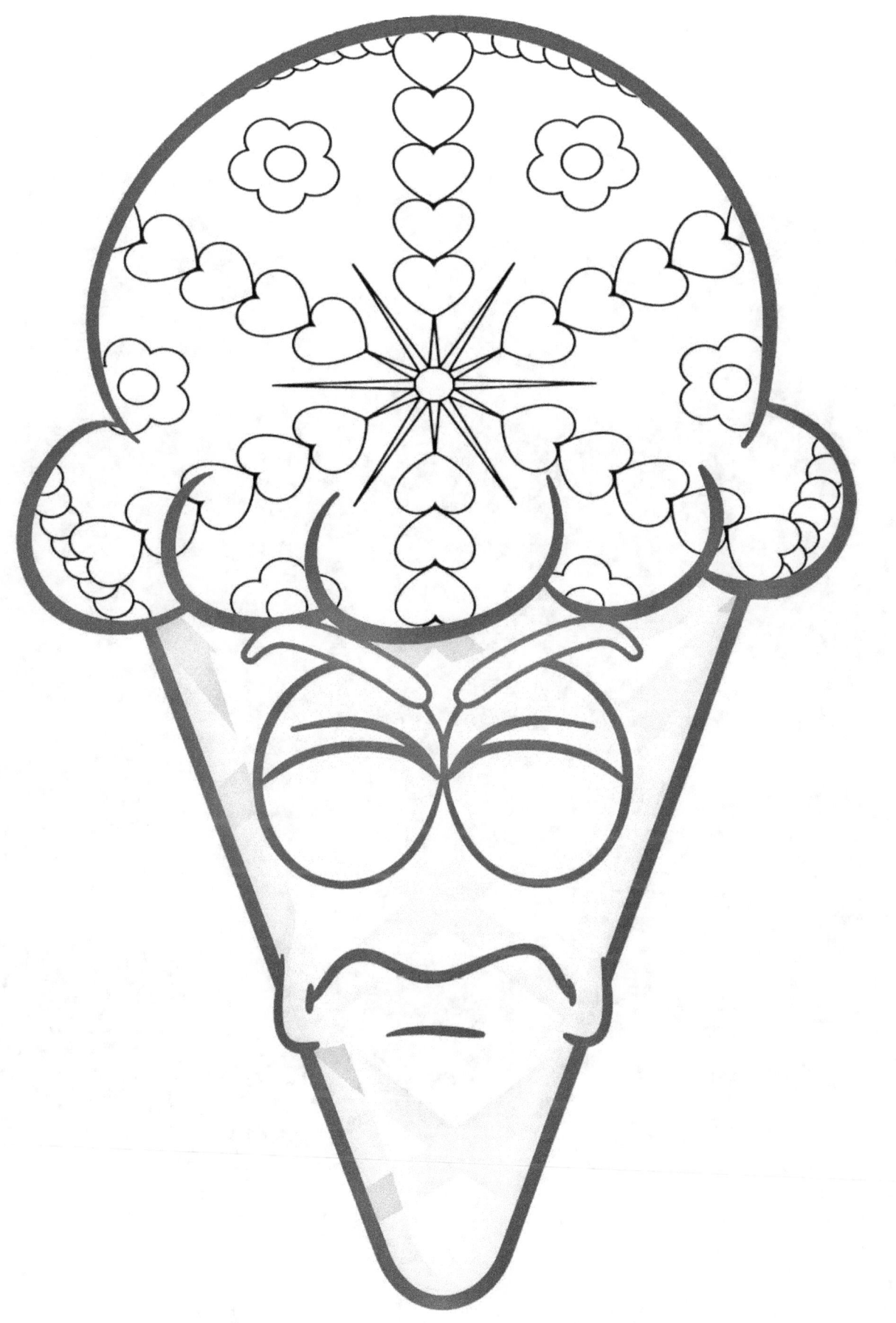

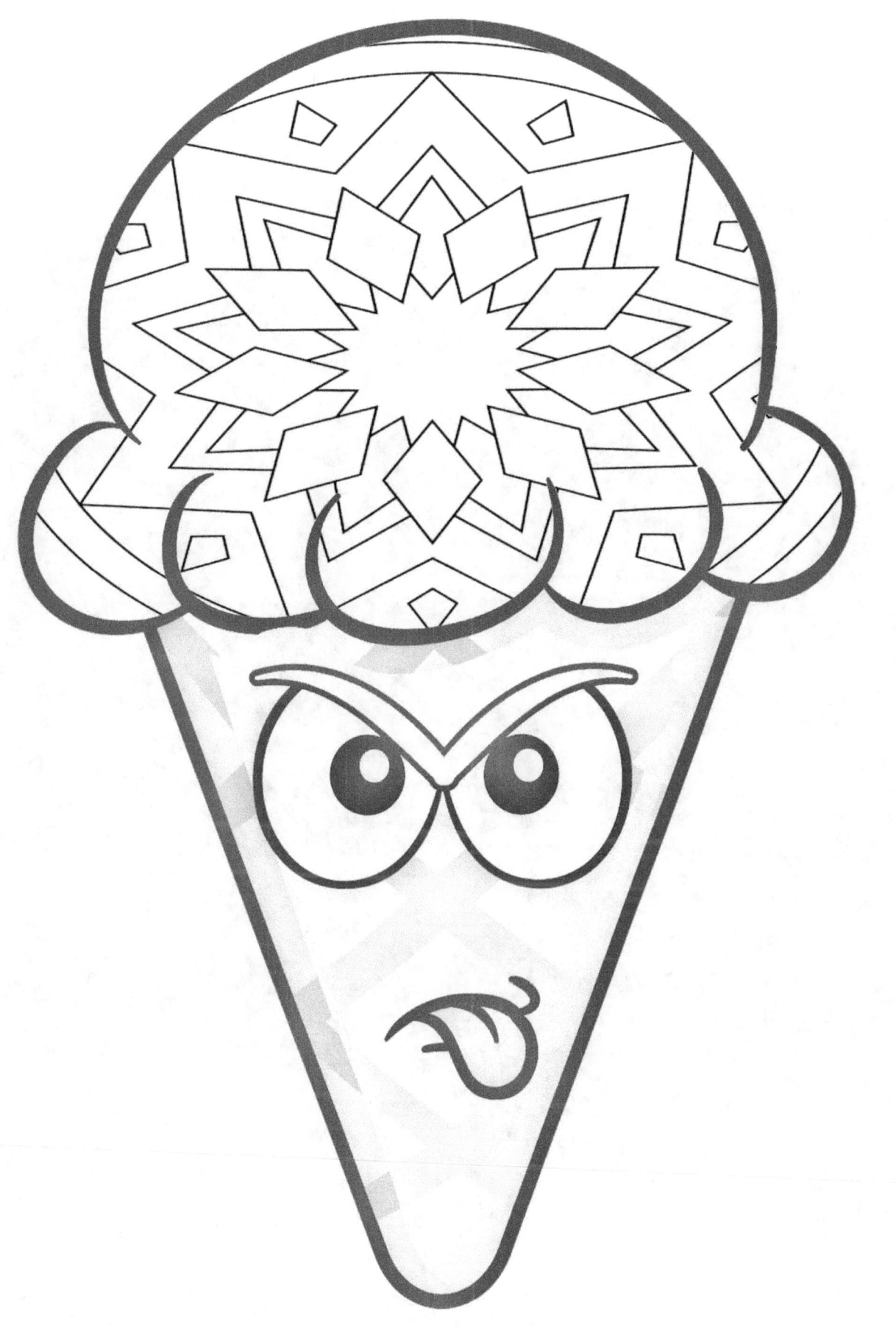

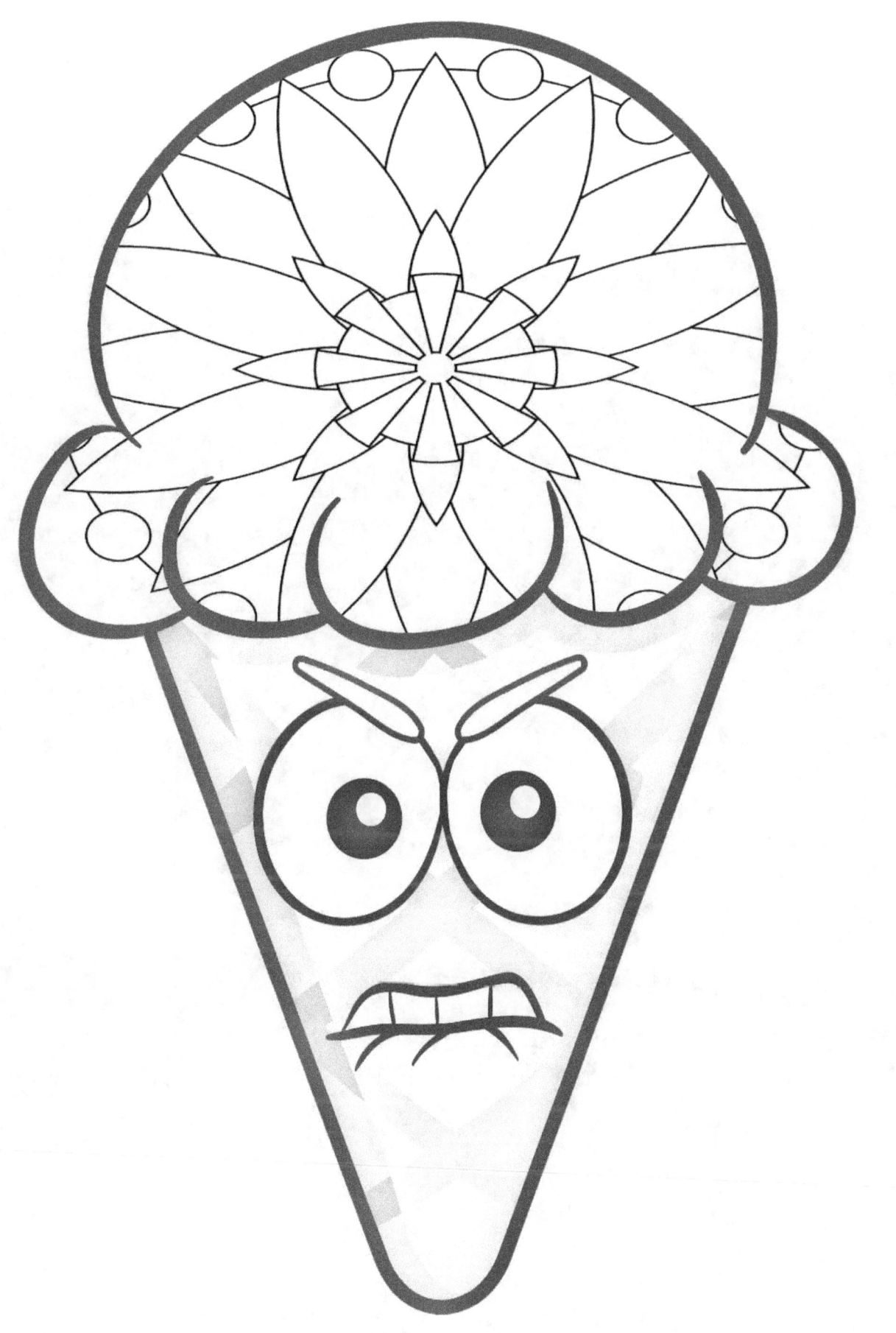

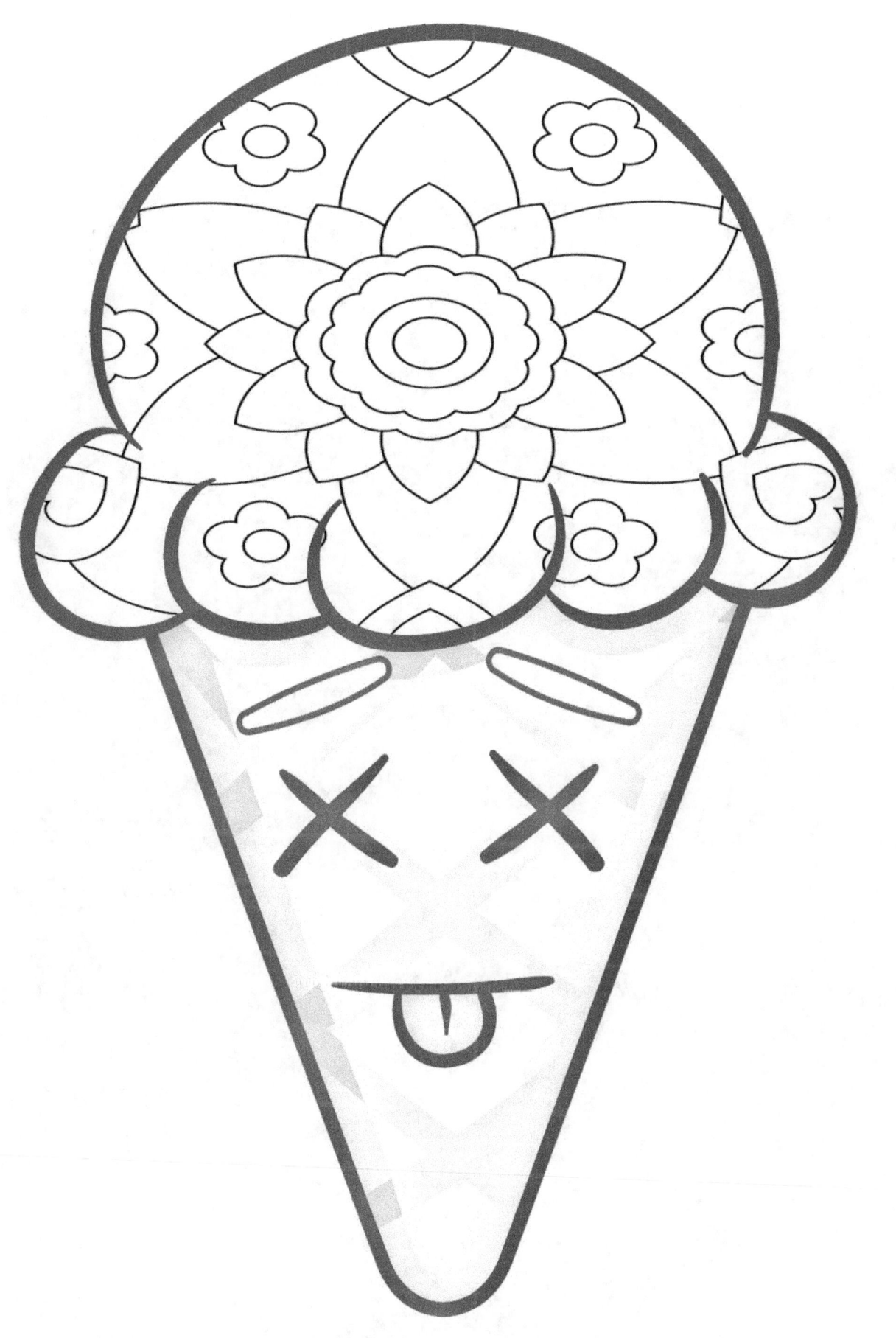

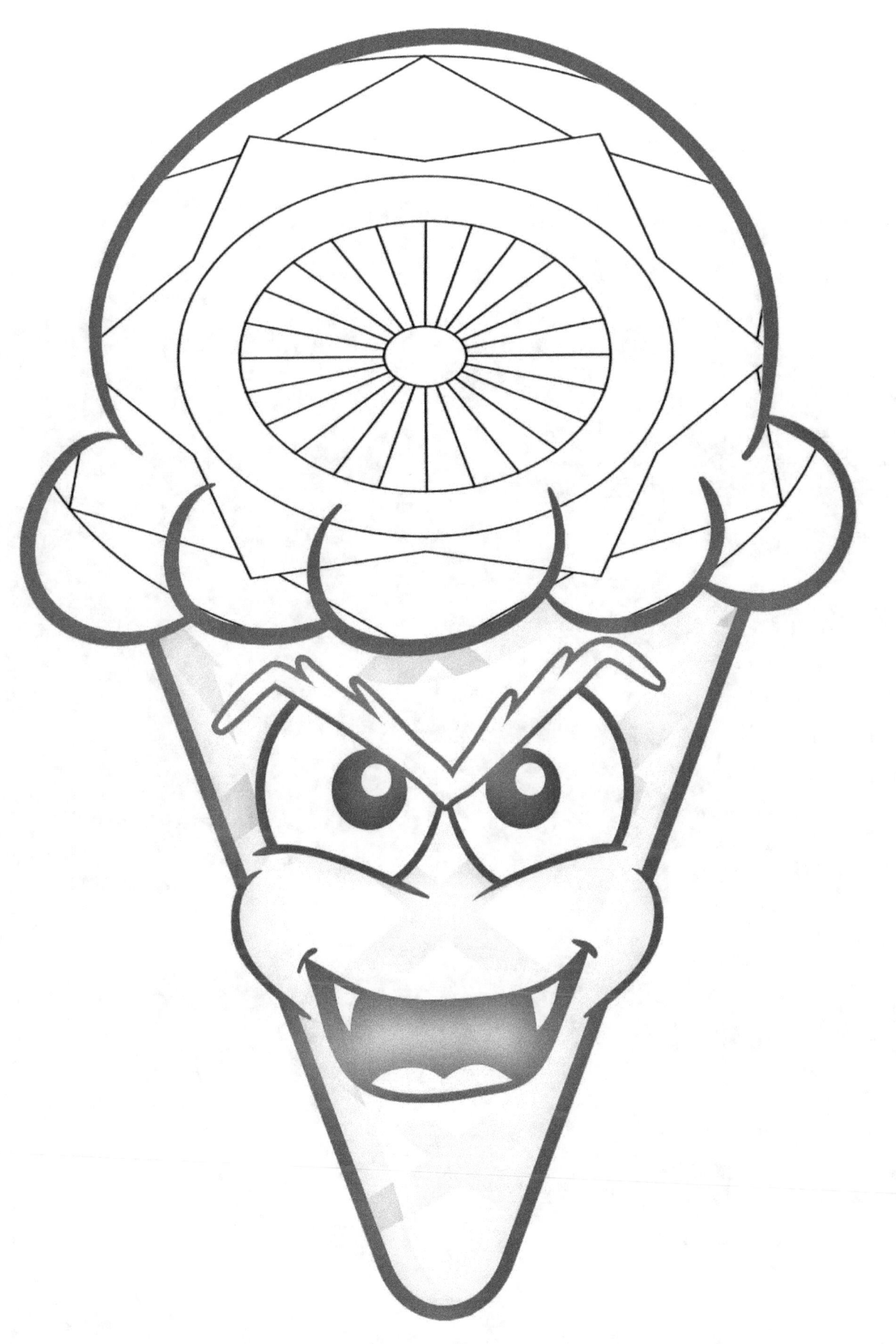

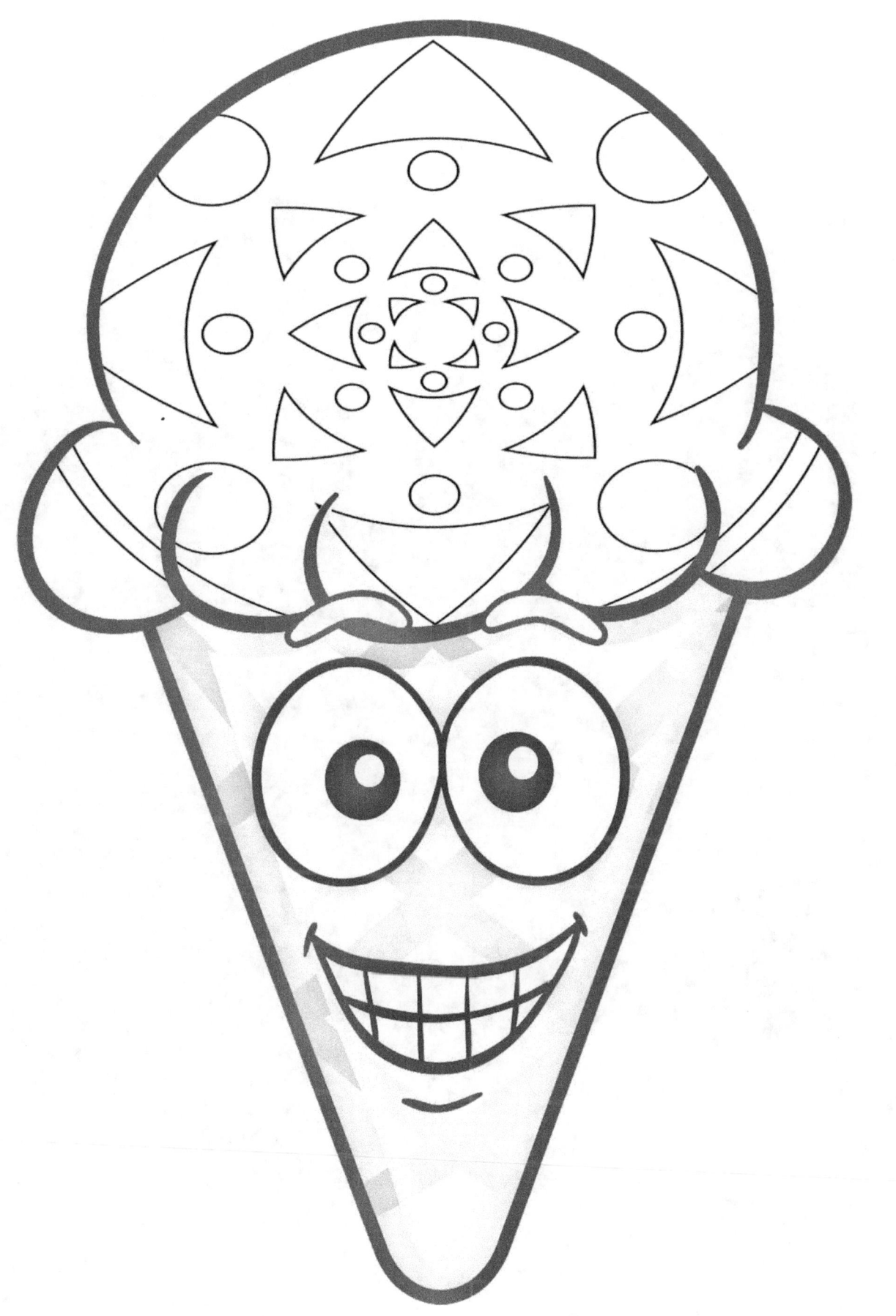

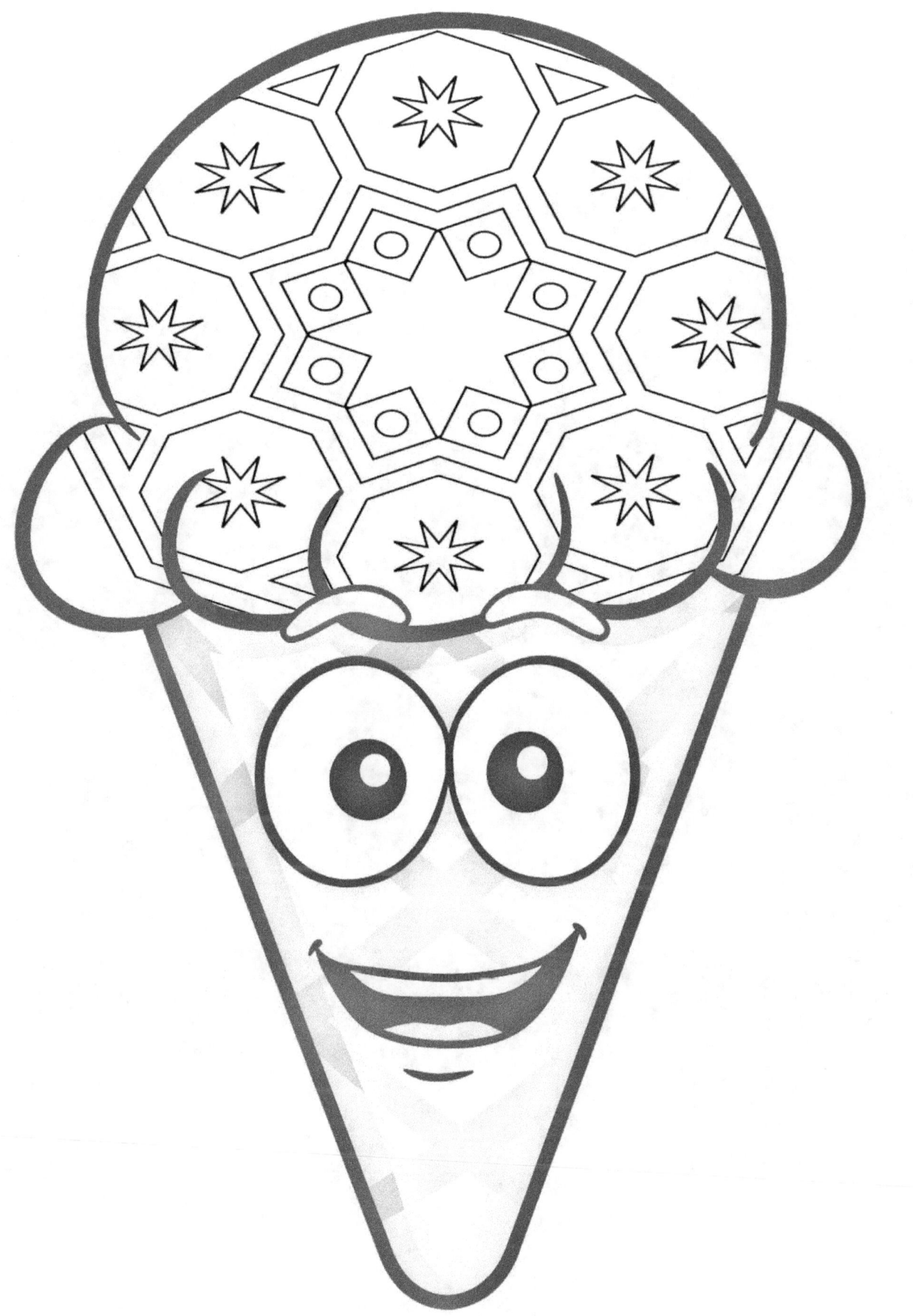

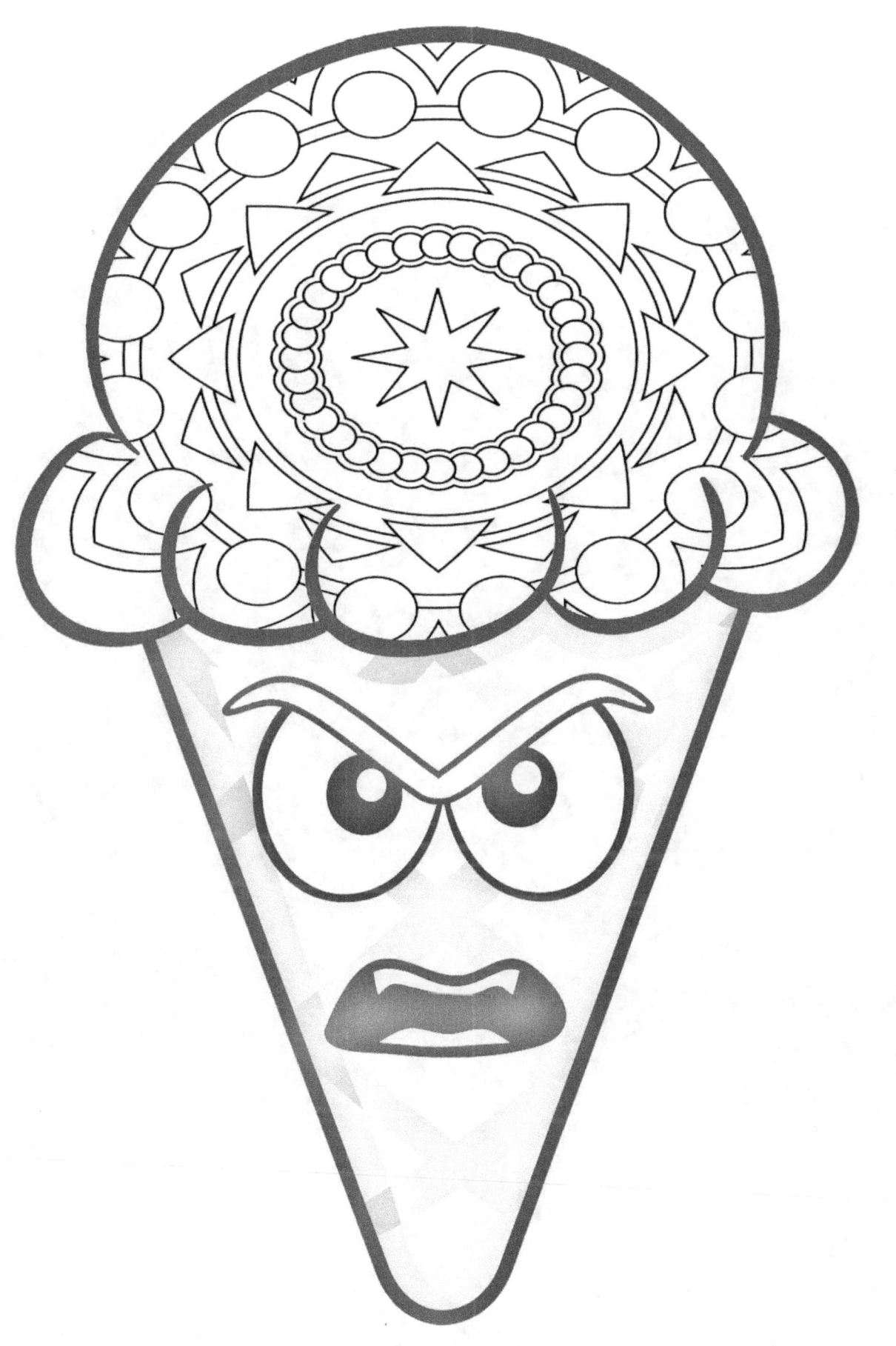

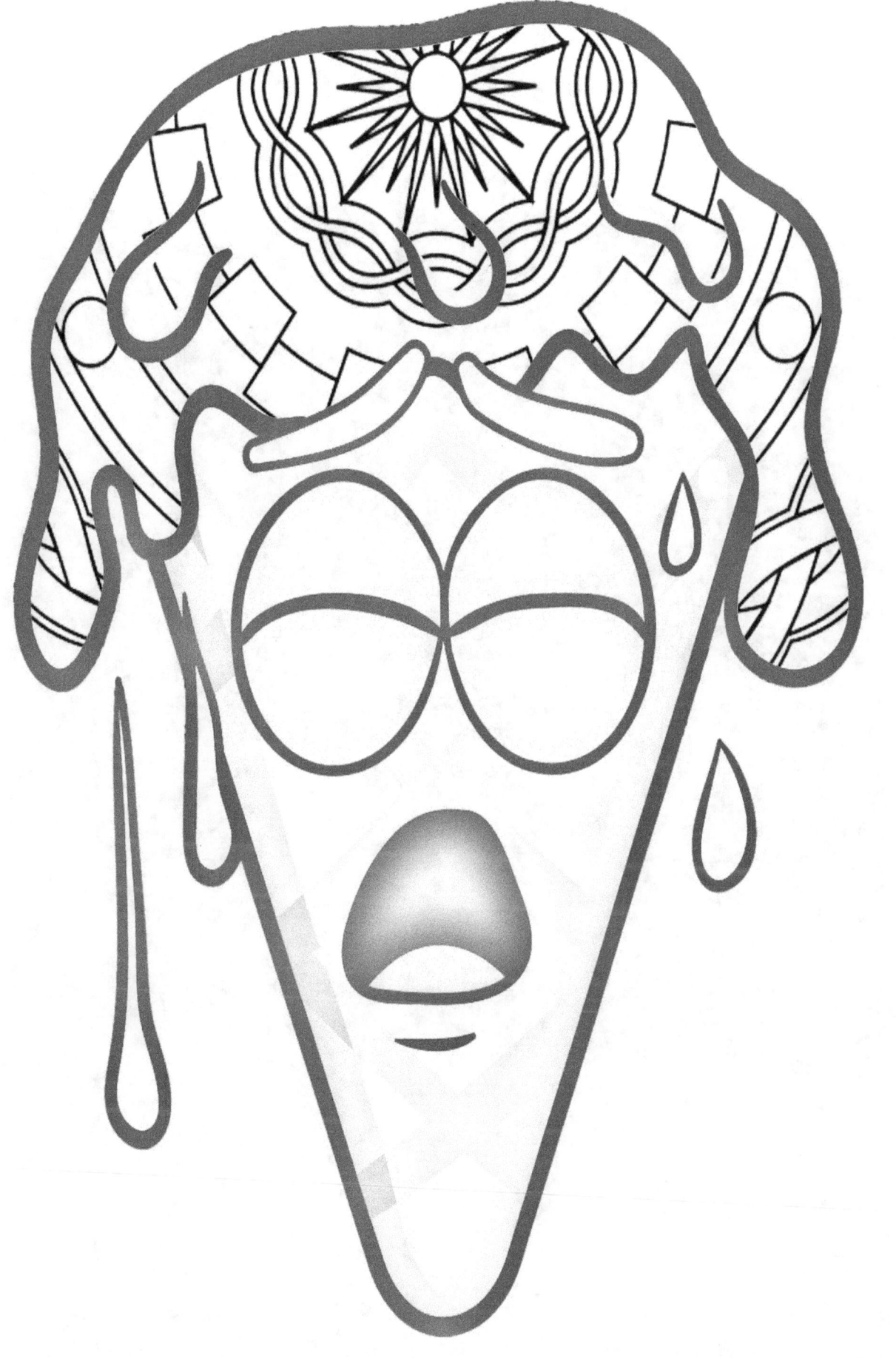

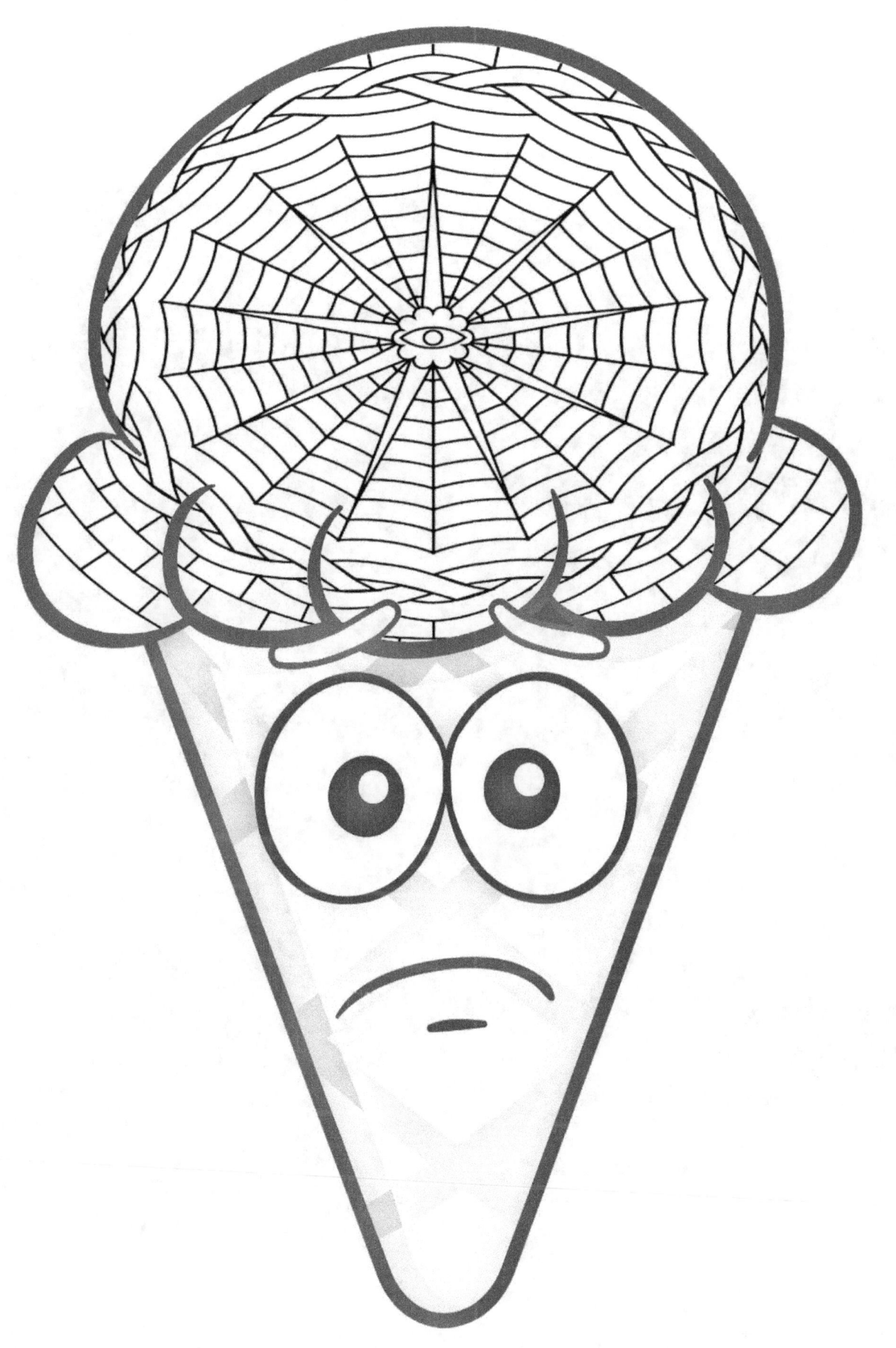

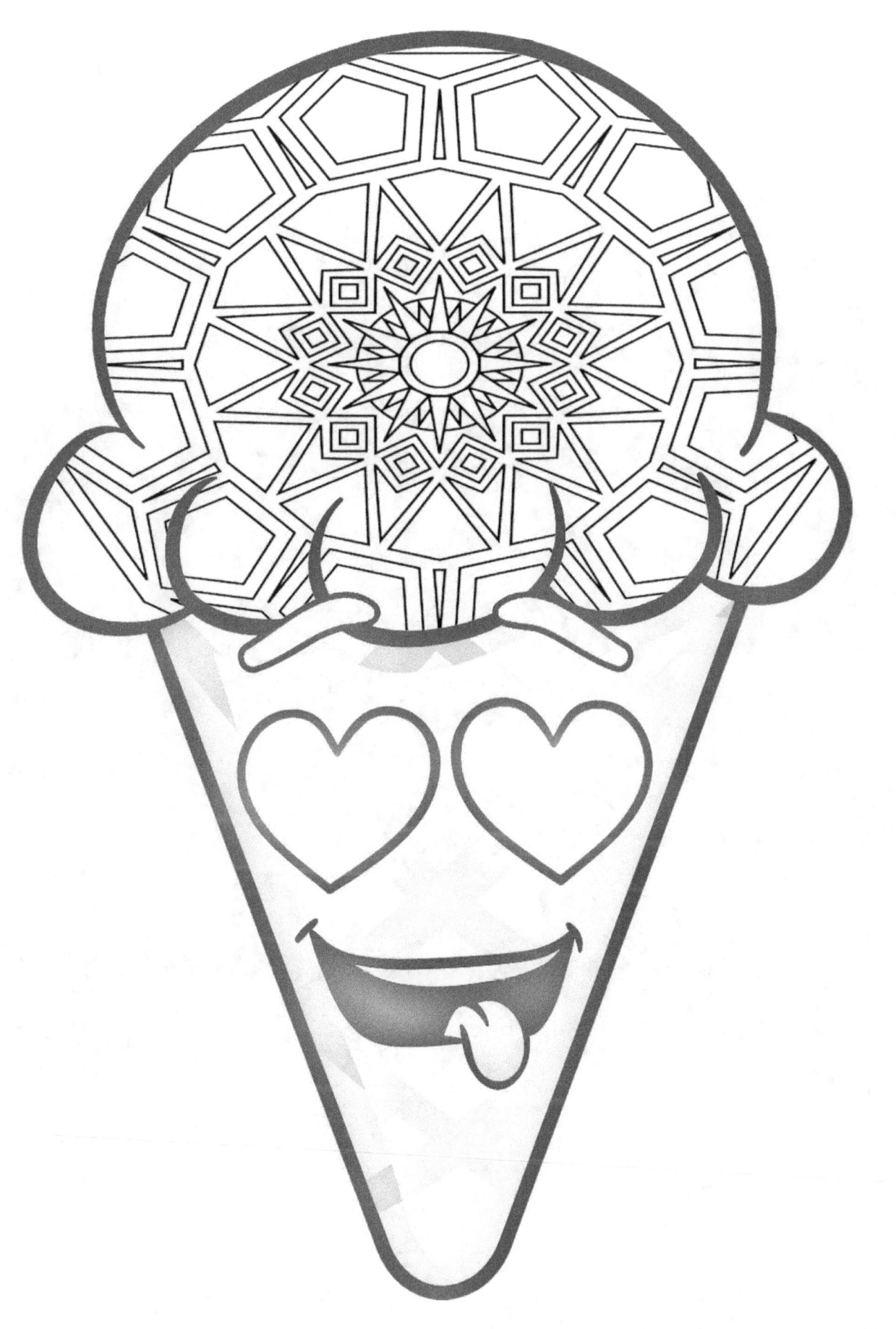

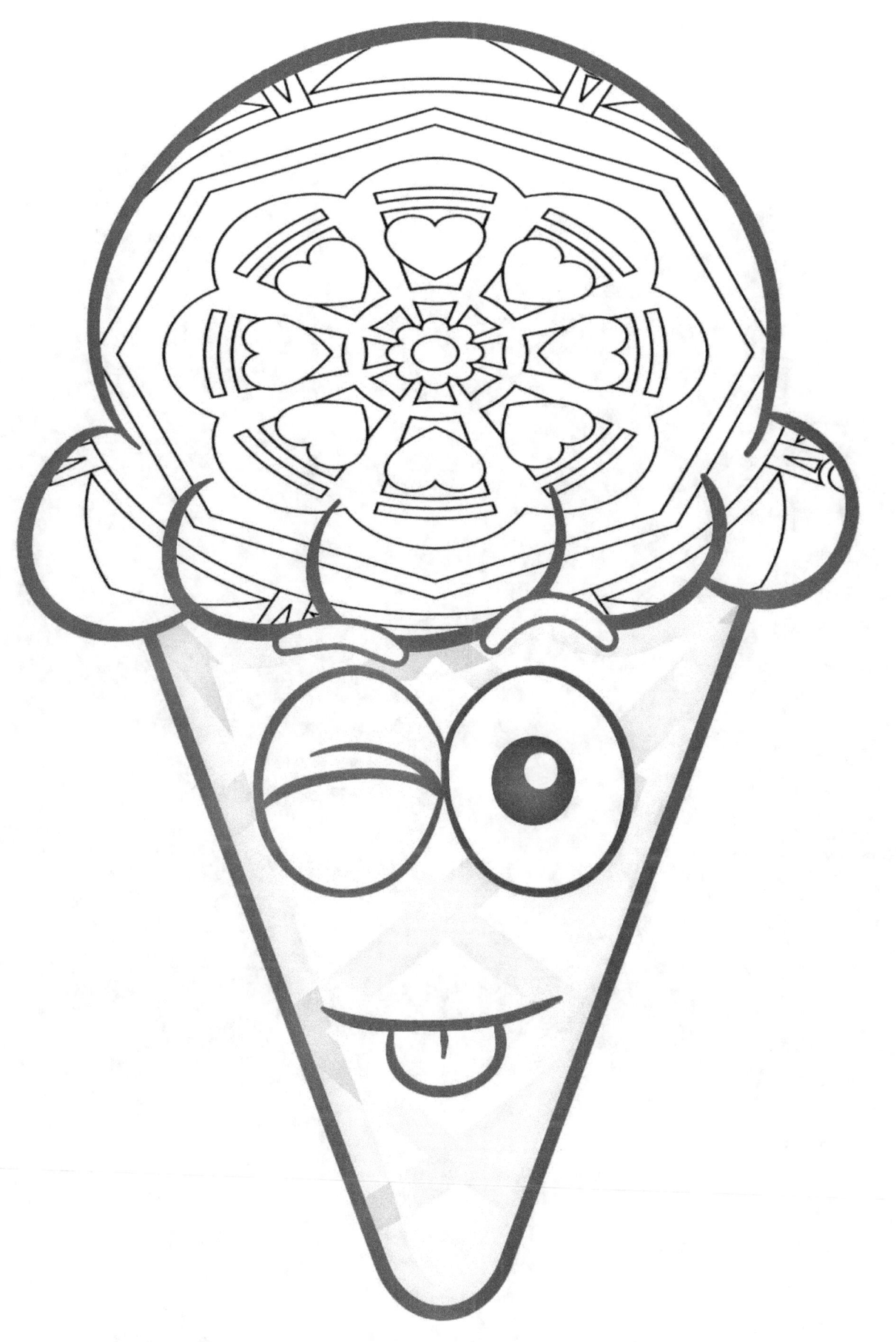

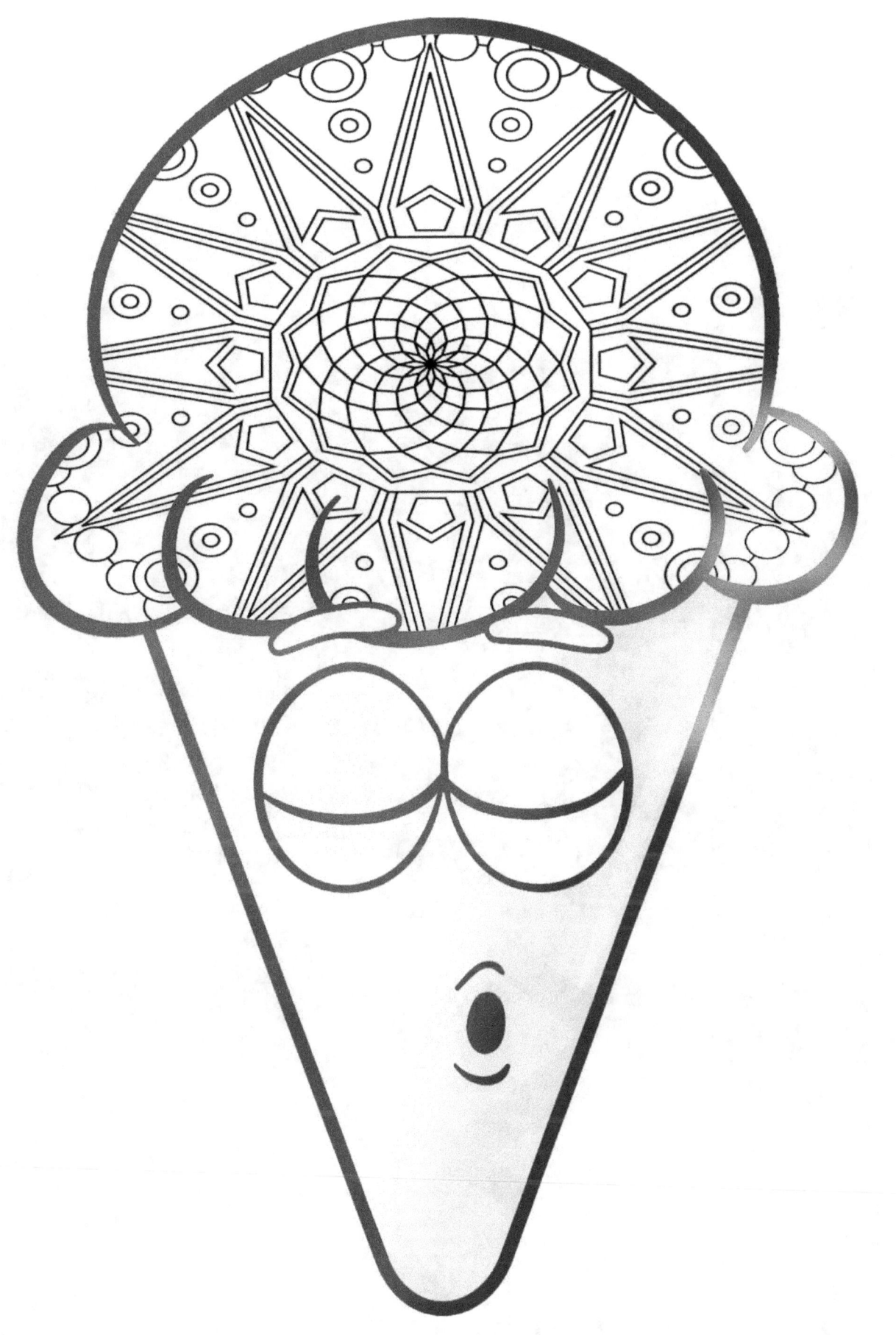

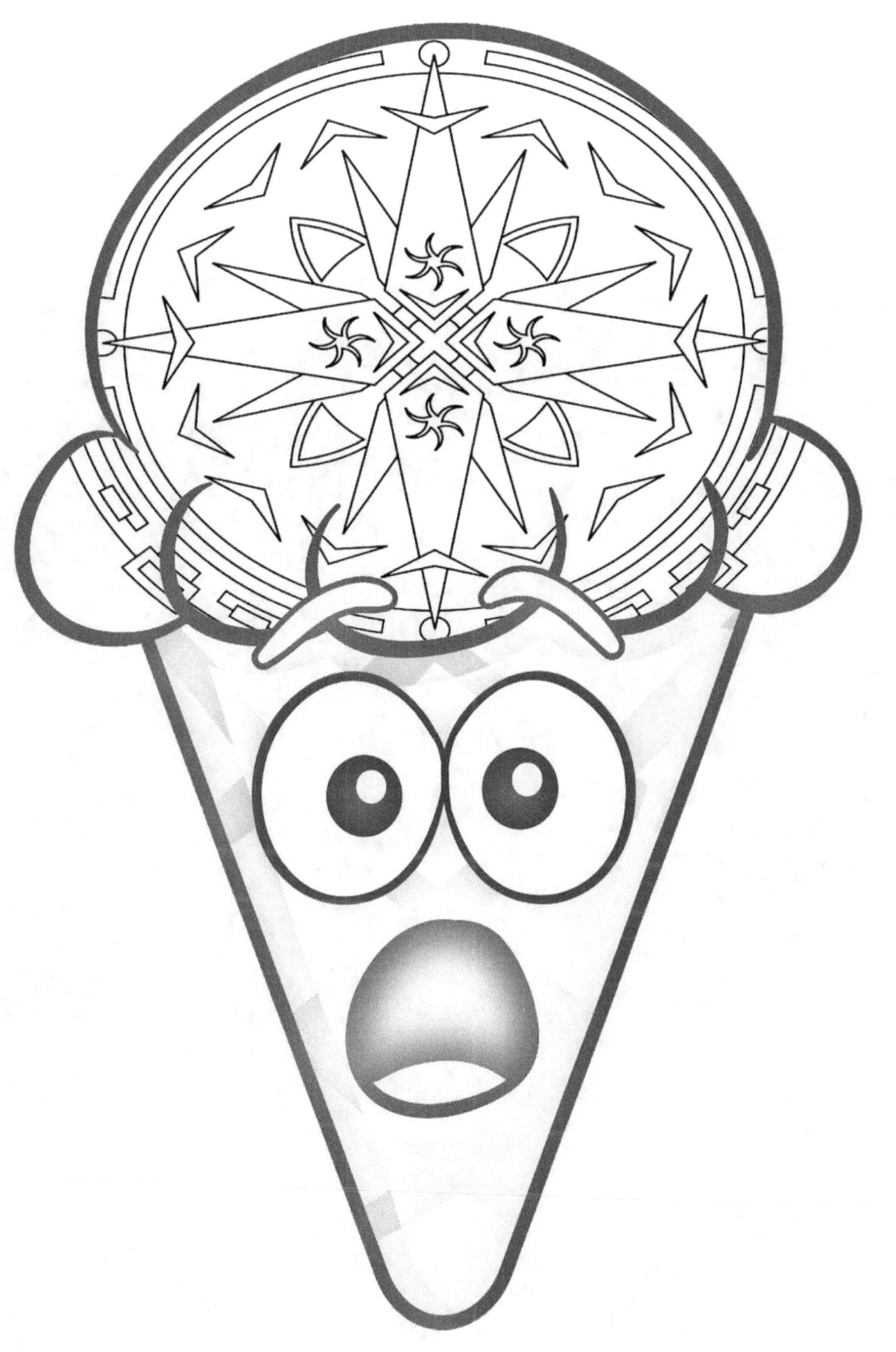

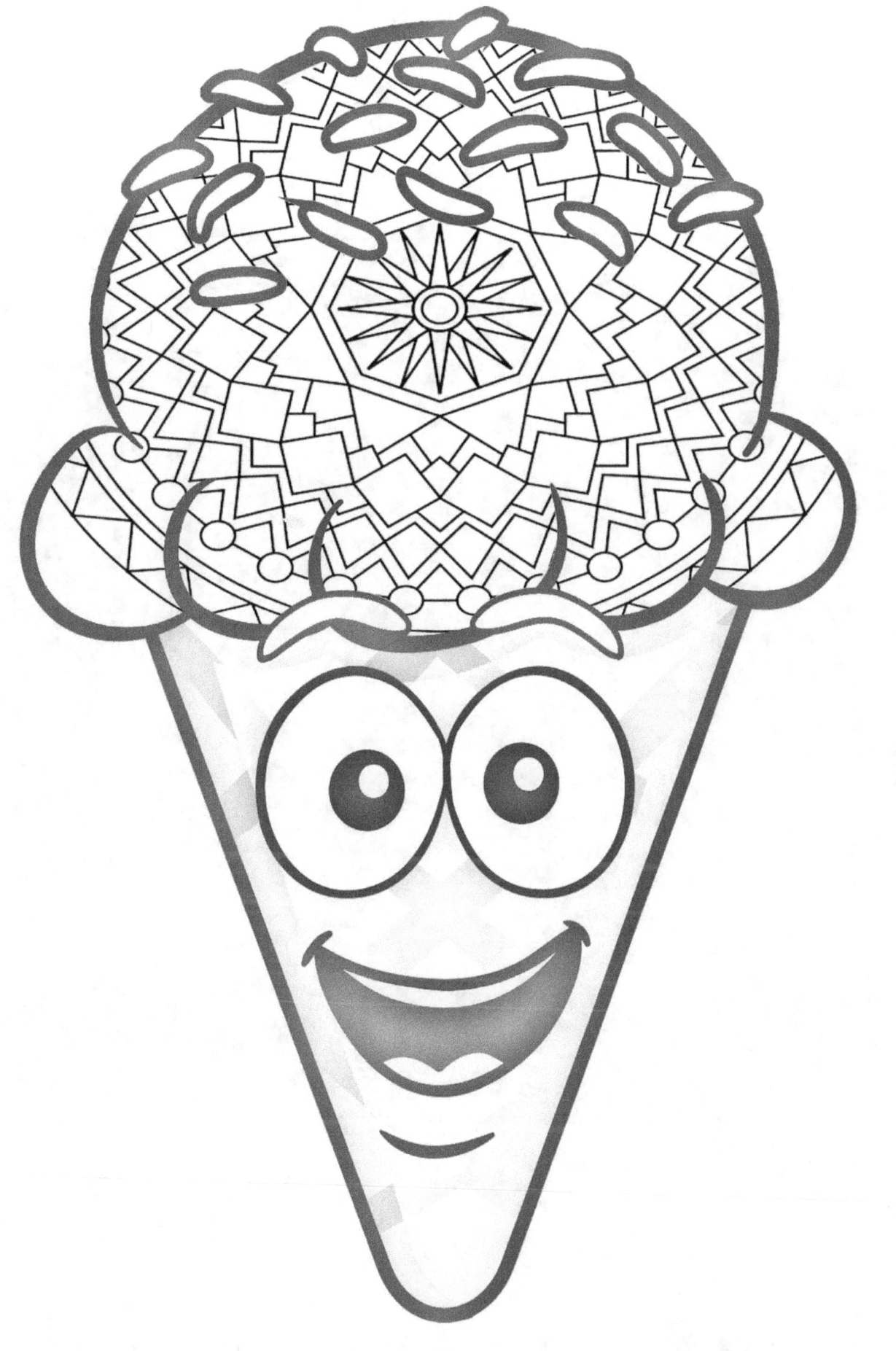

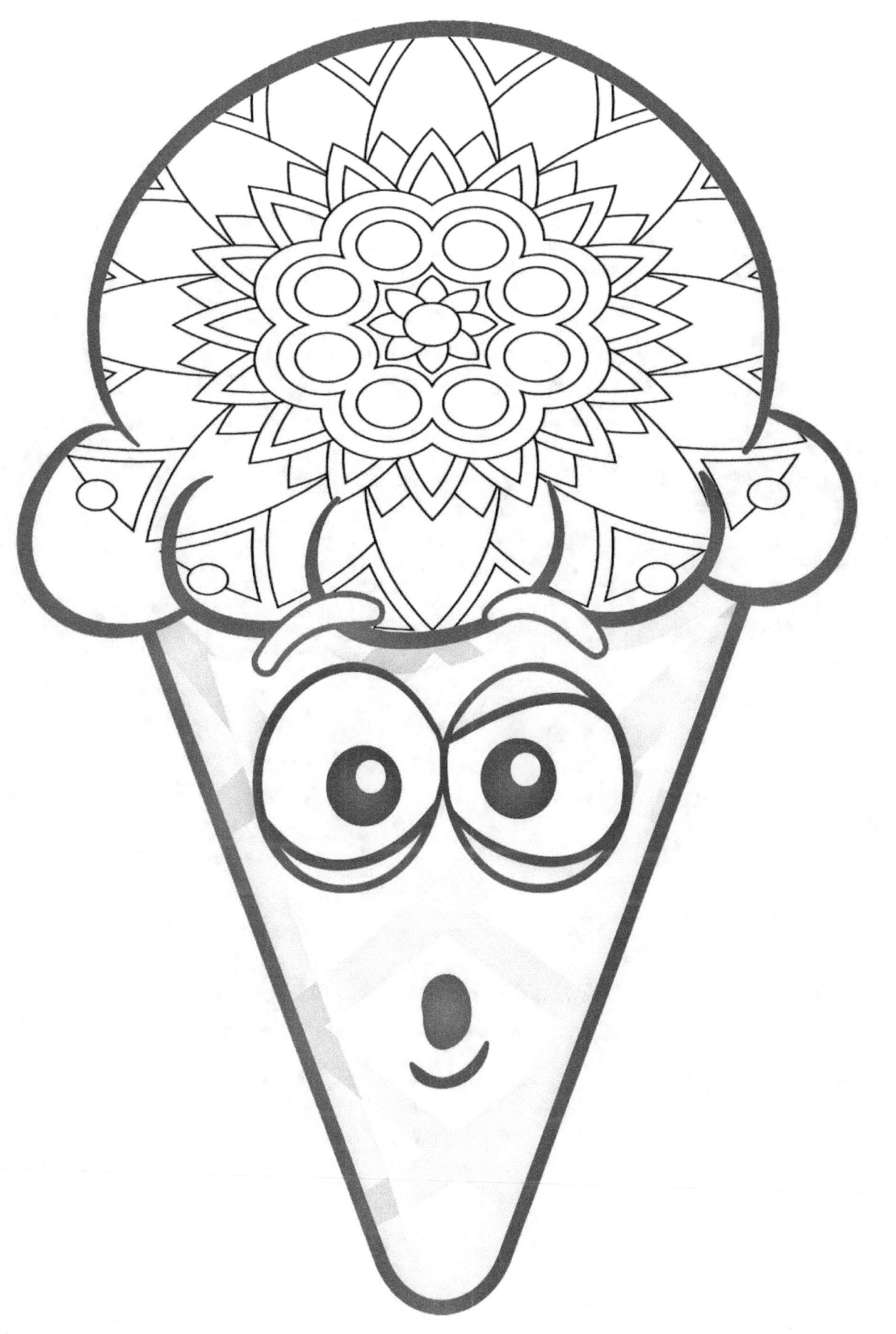

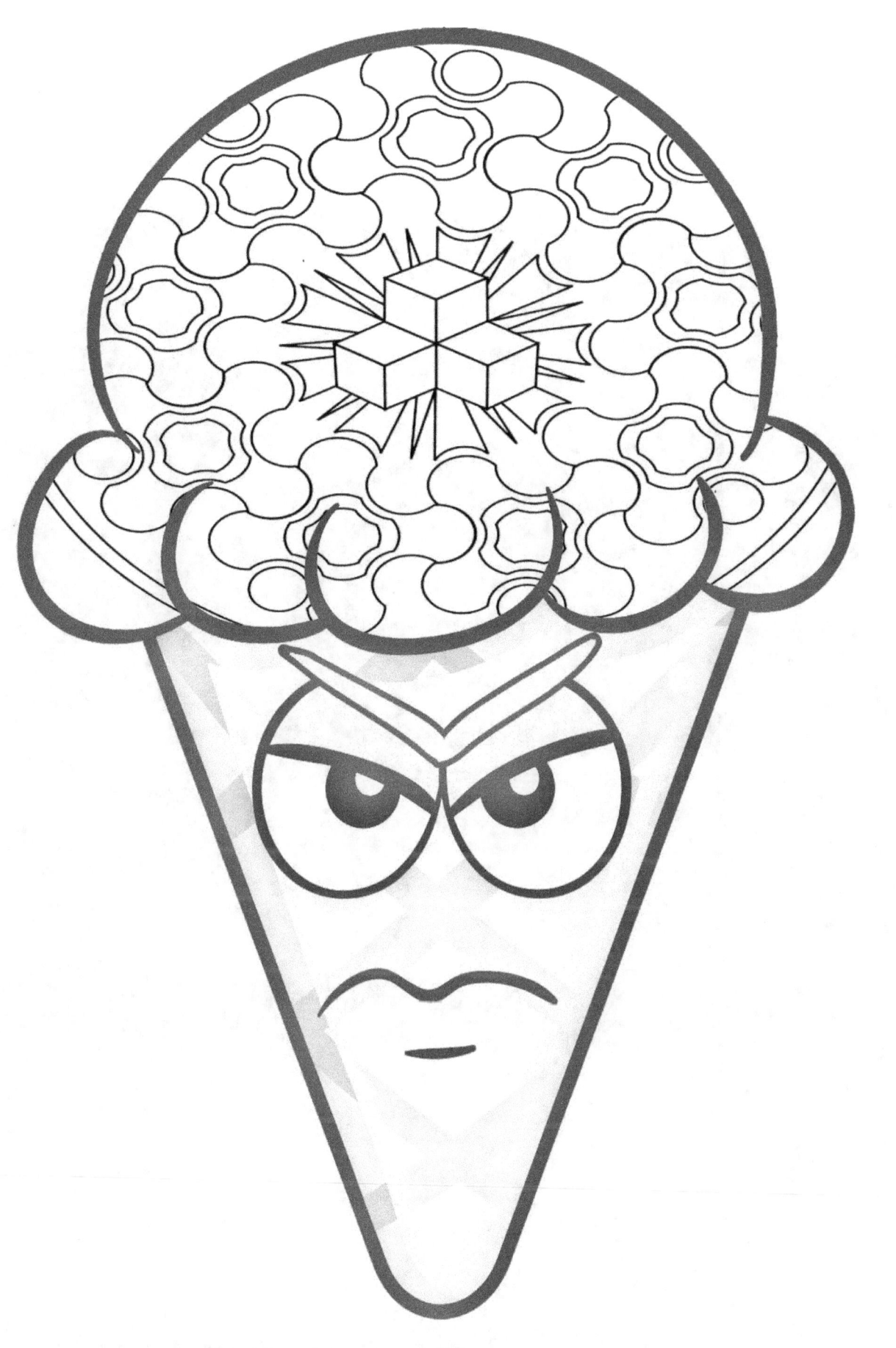

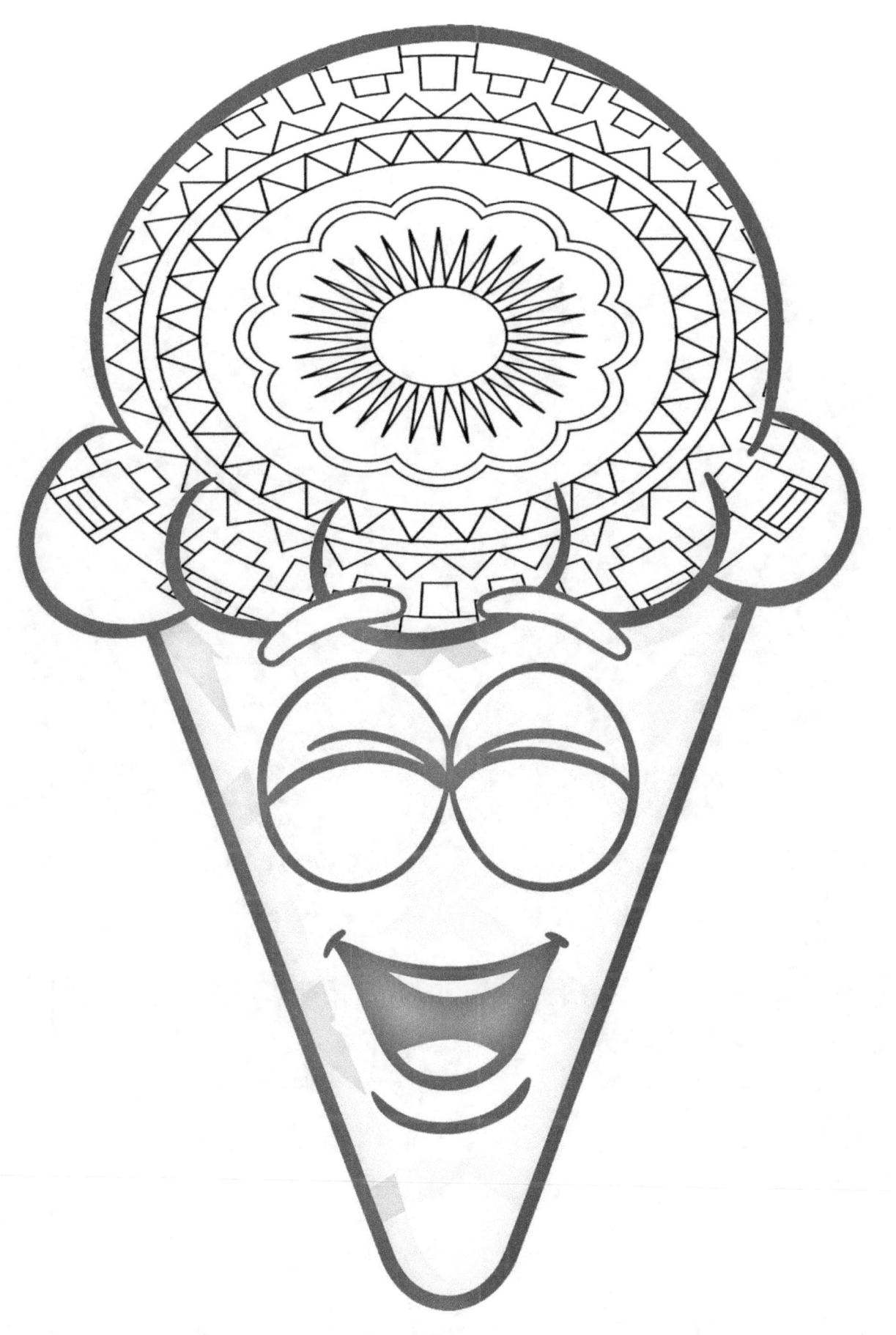

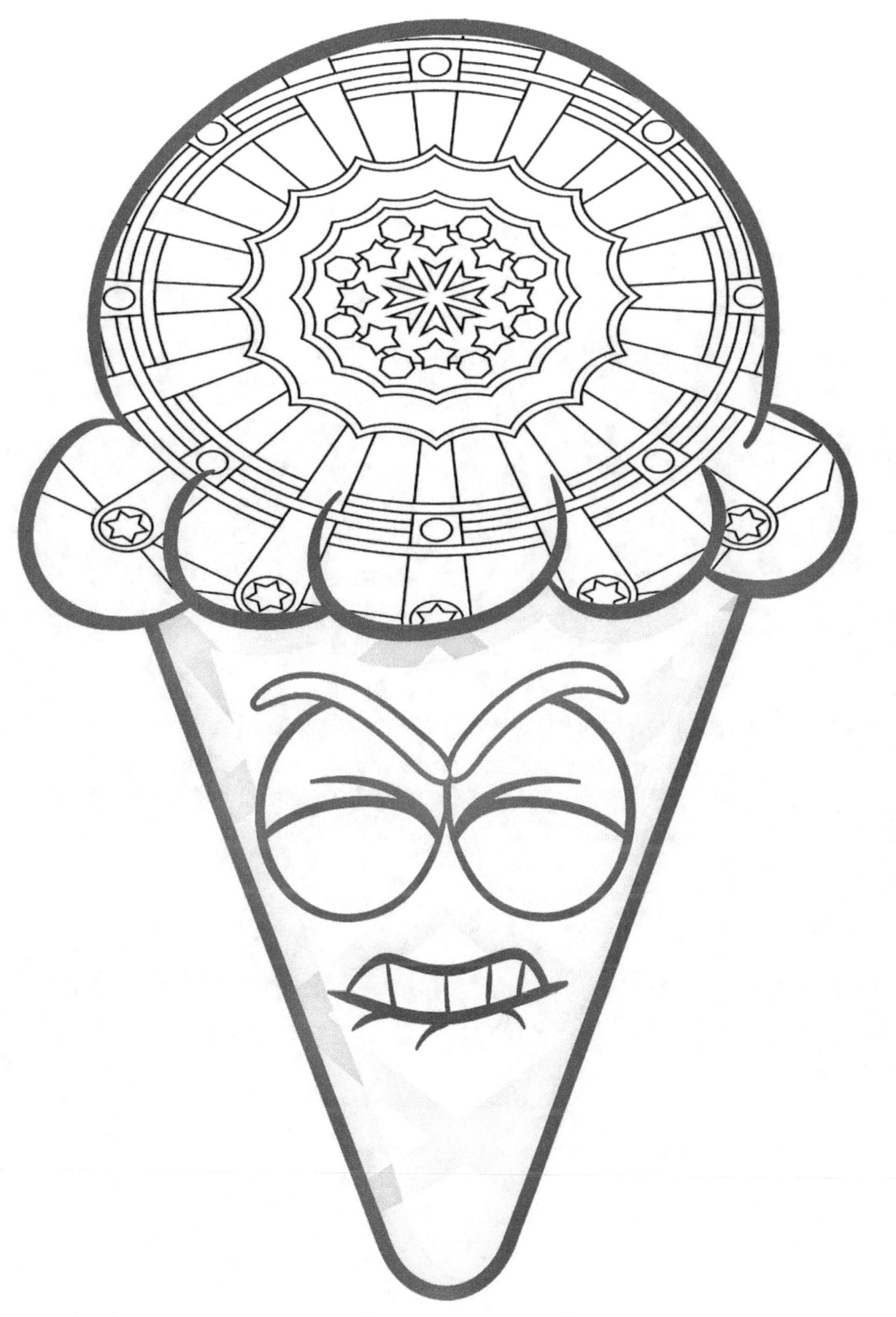

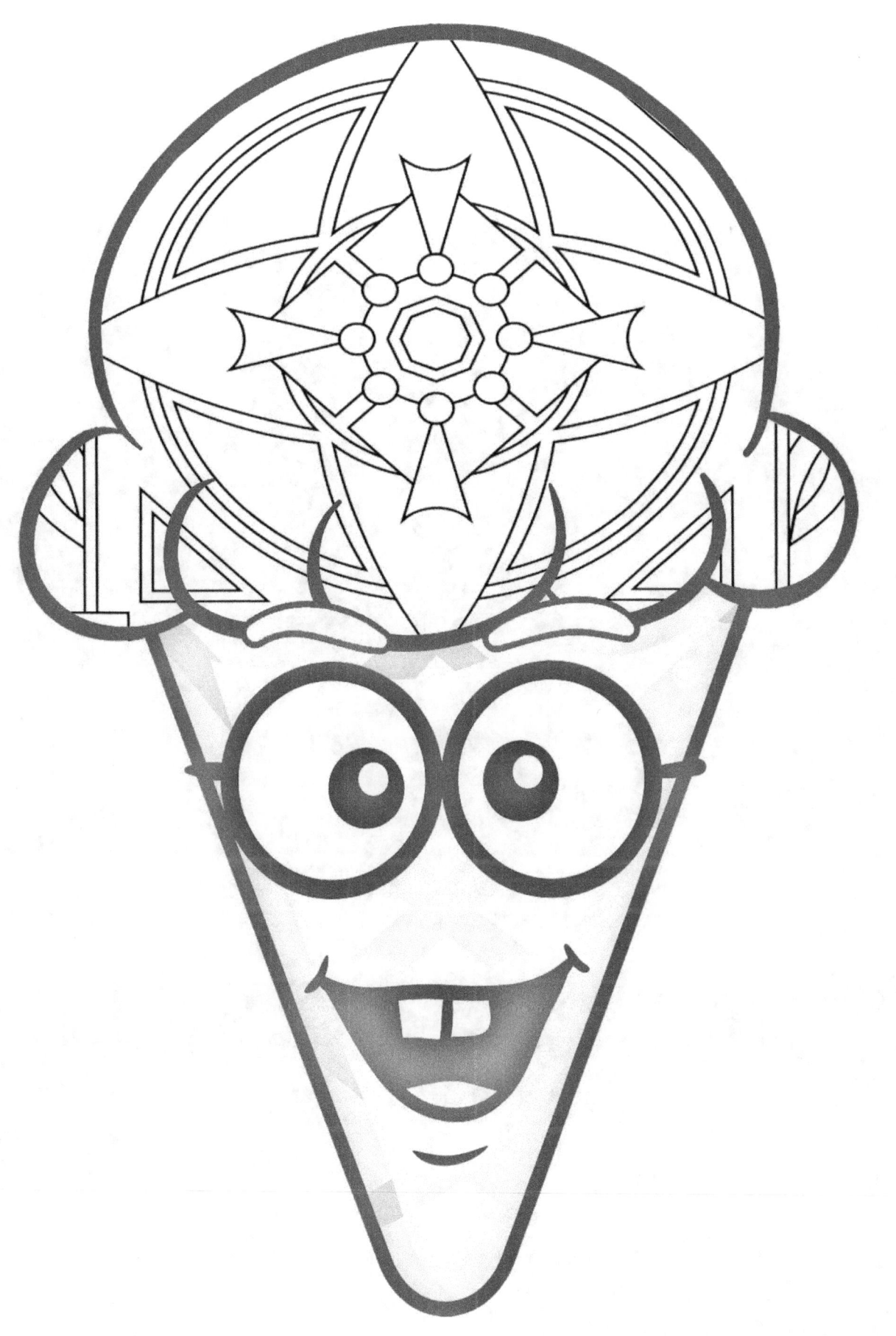

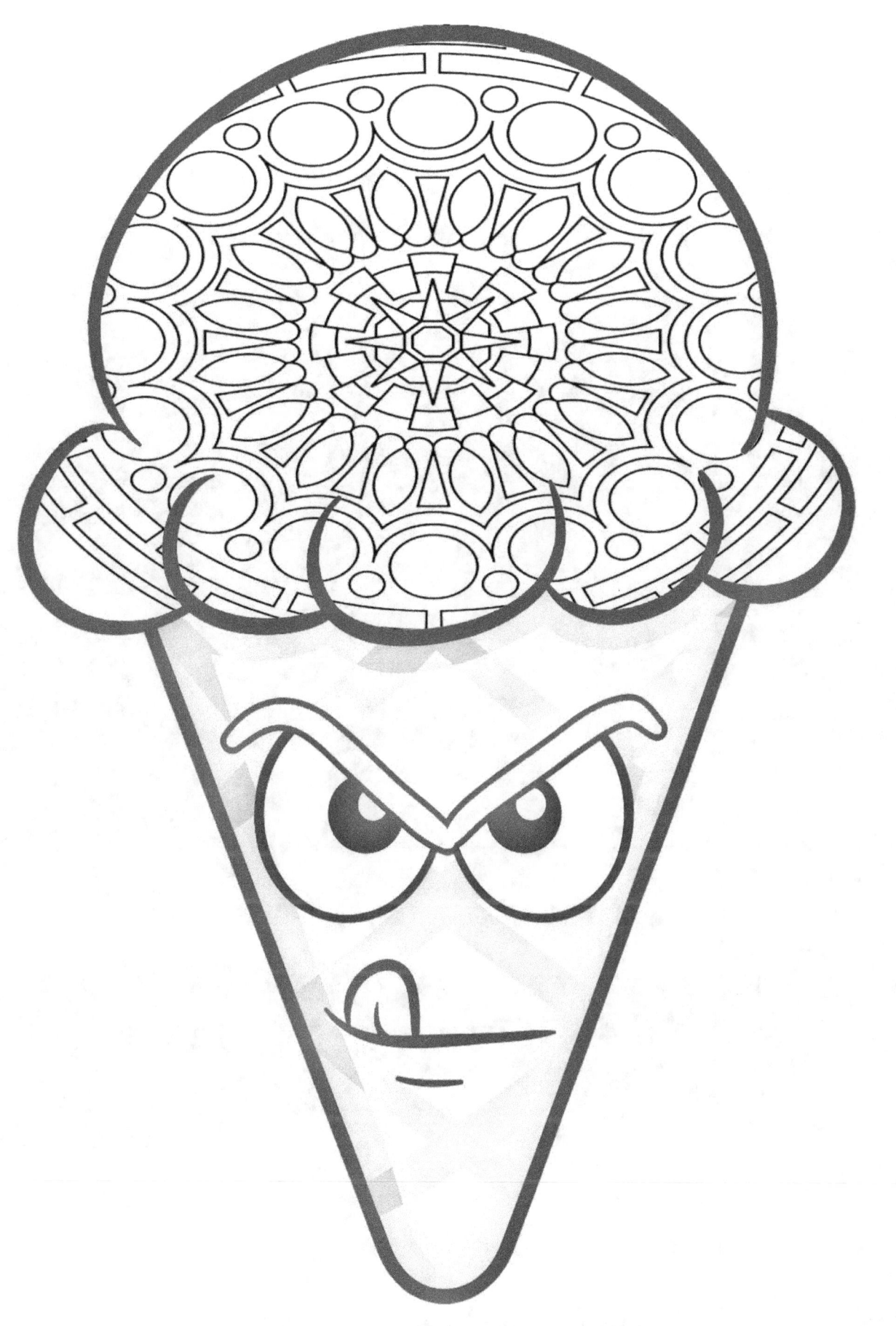

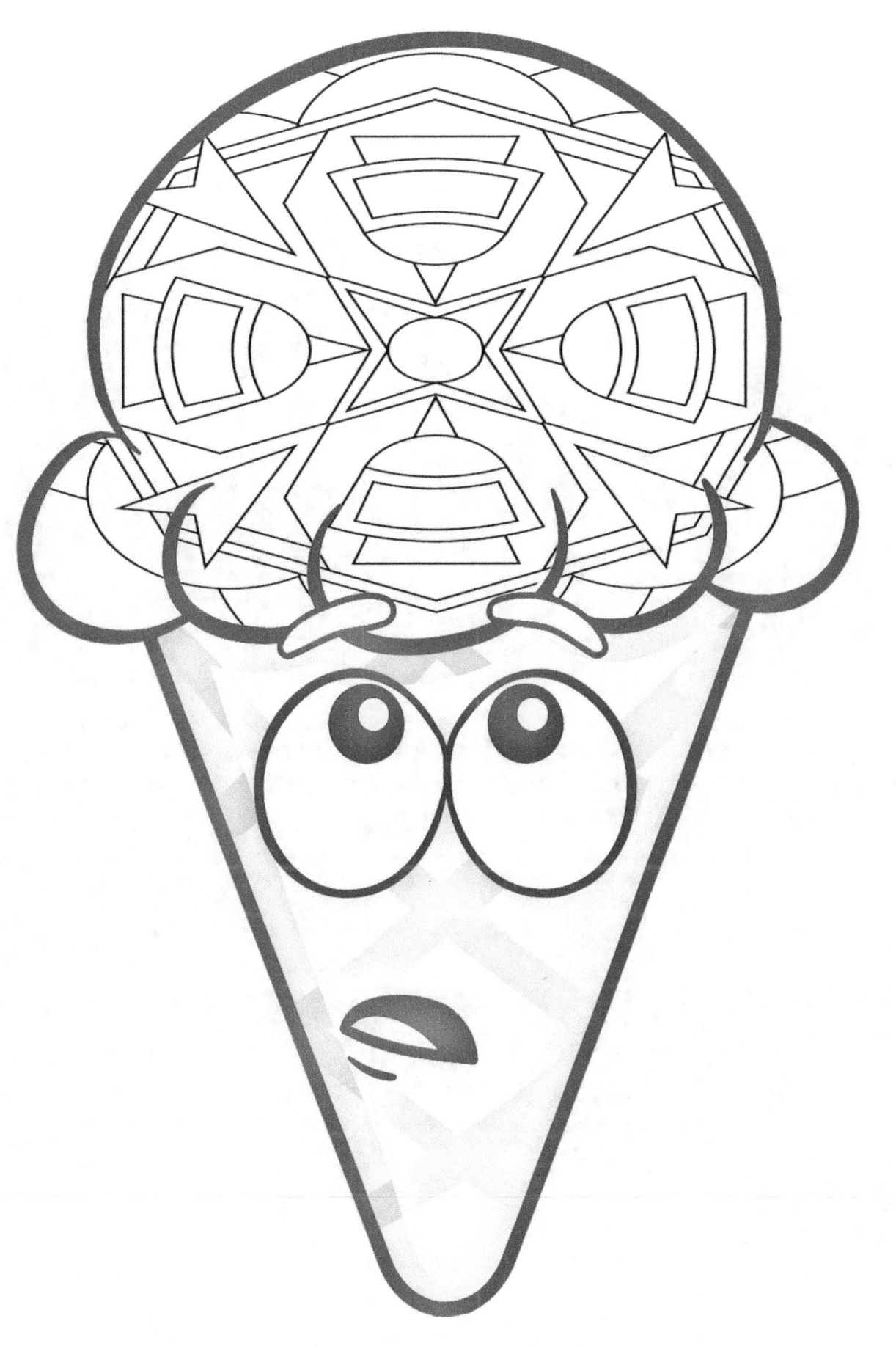

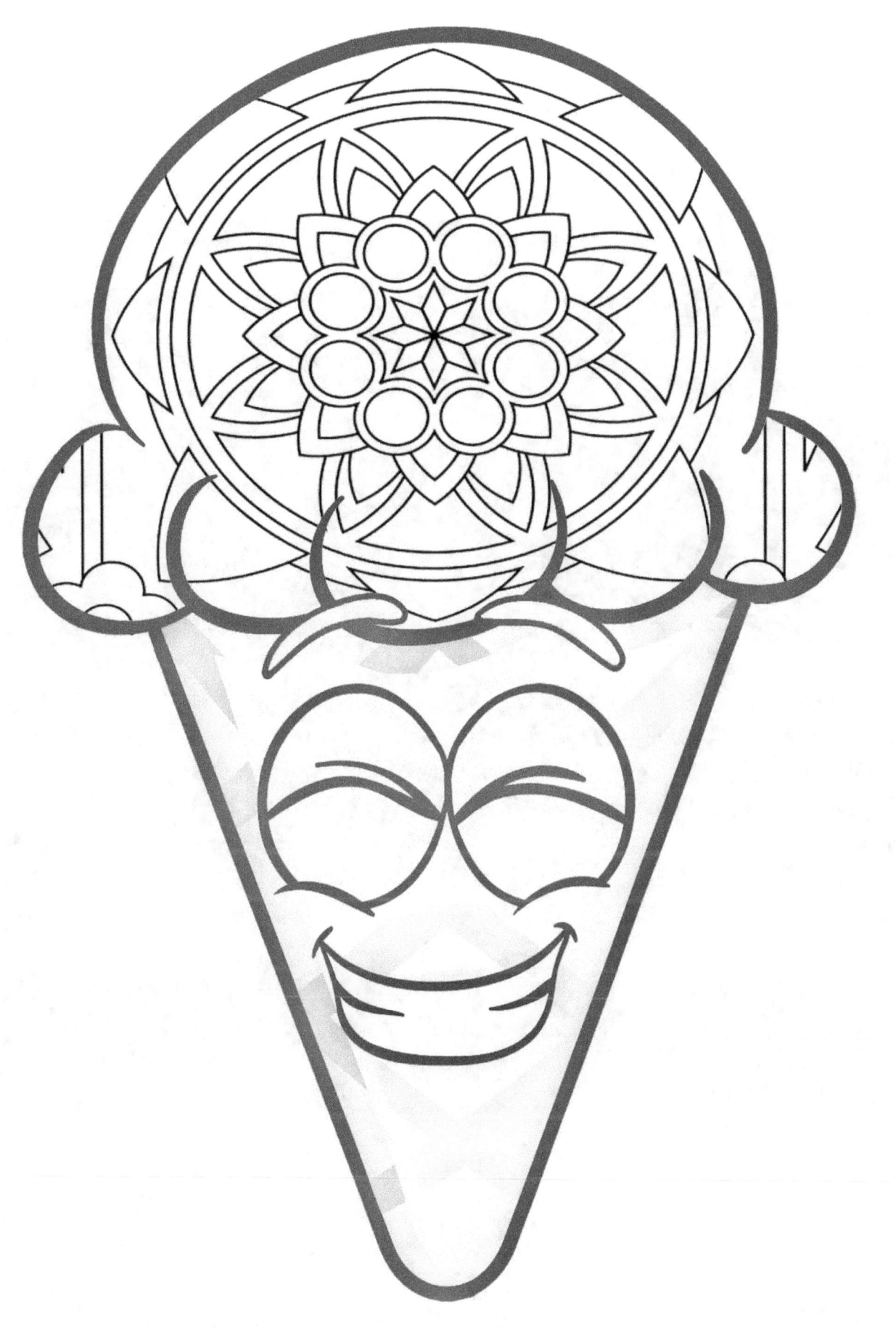

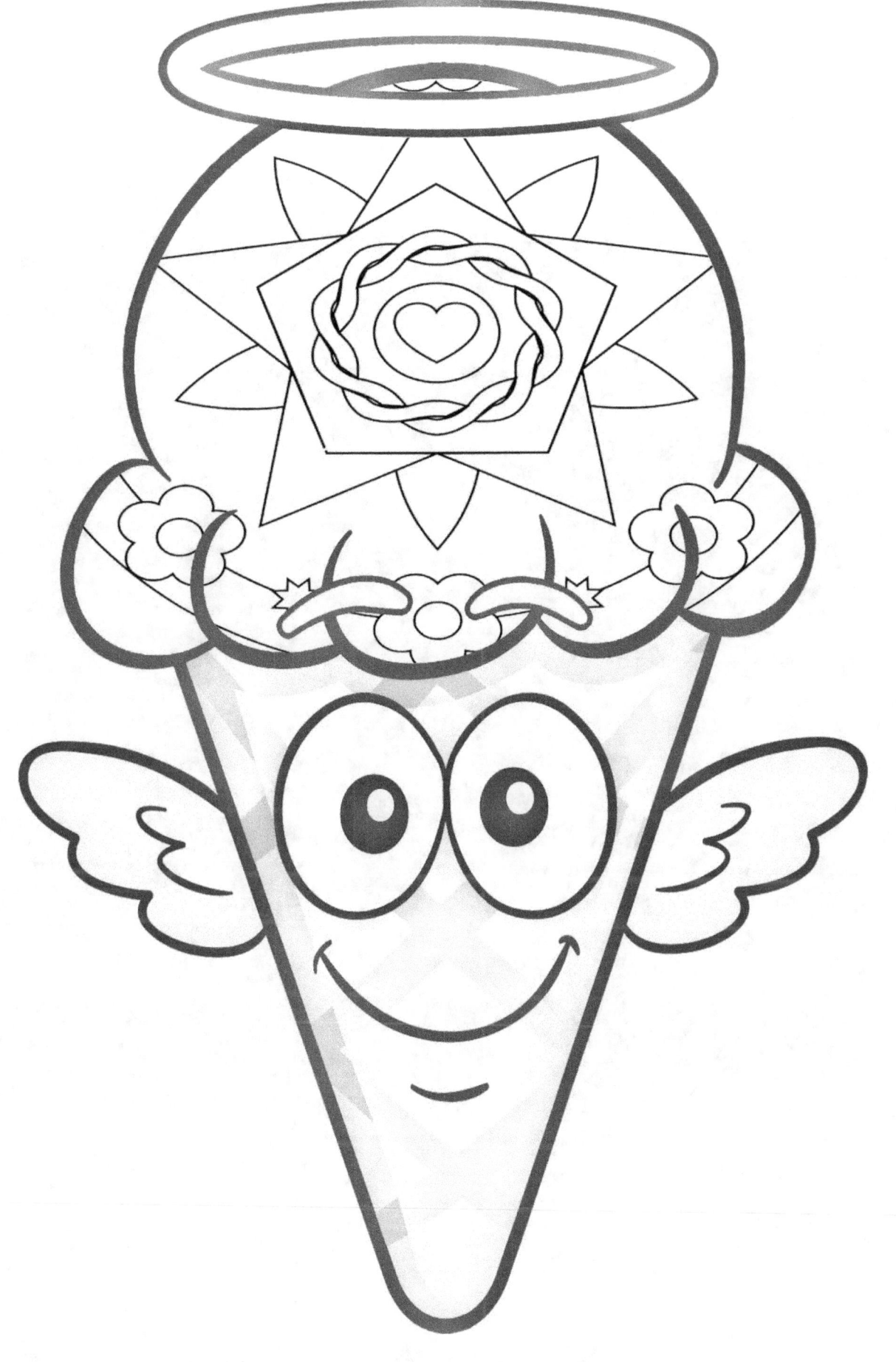

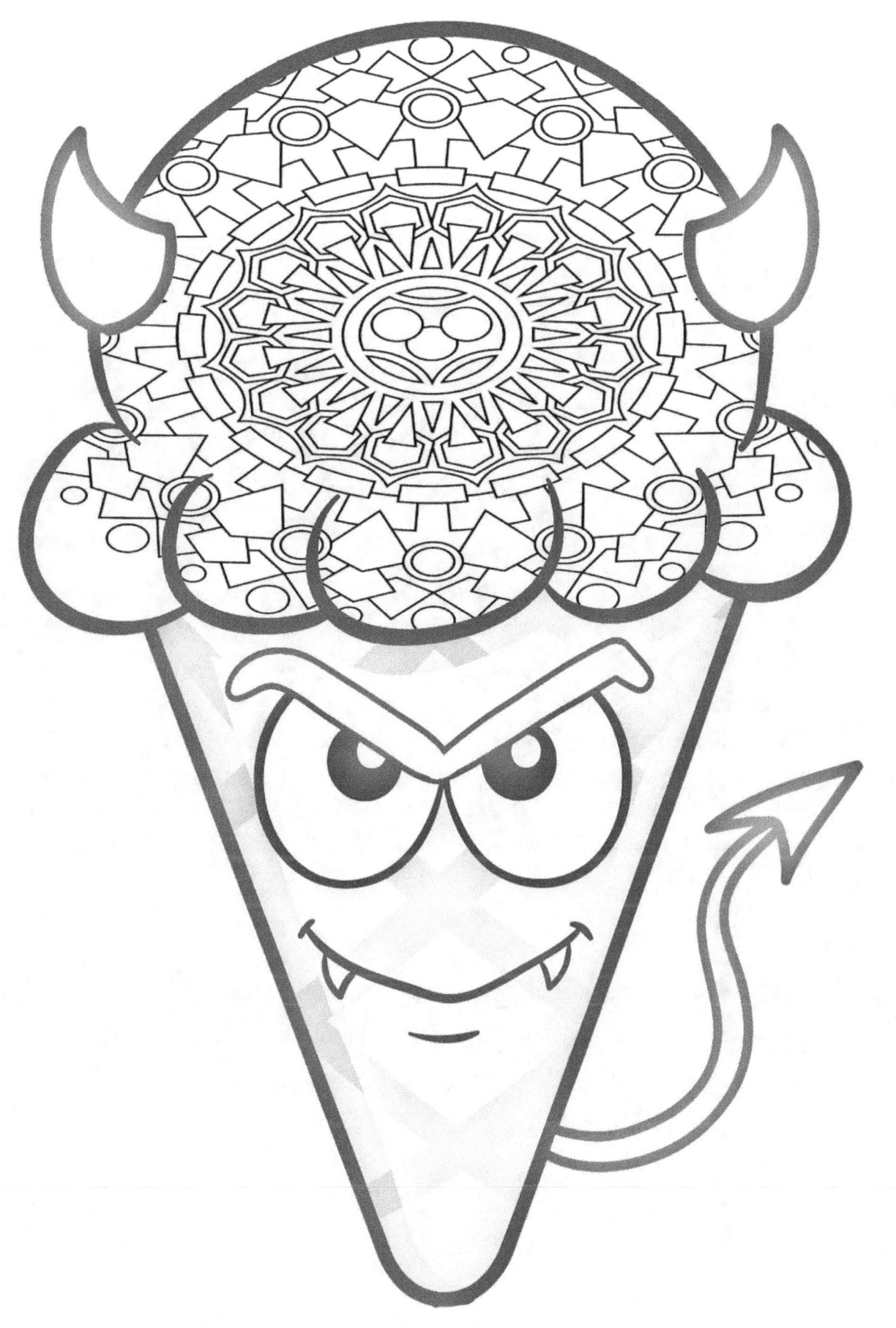

Copyright © 2015 Mad House Coloring

All Rights Reserved Worldwide

The Totally MAD HOUSE COLORING BOOK

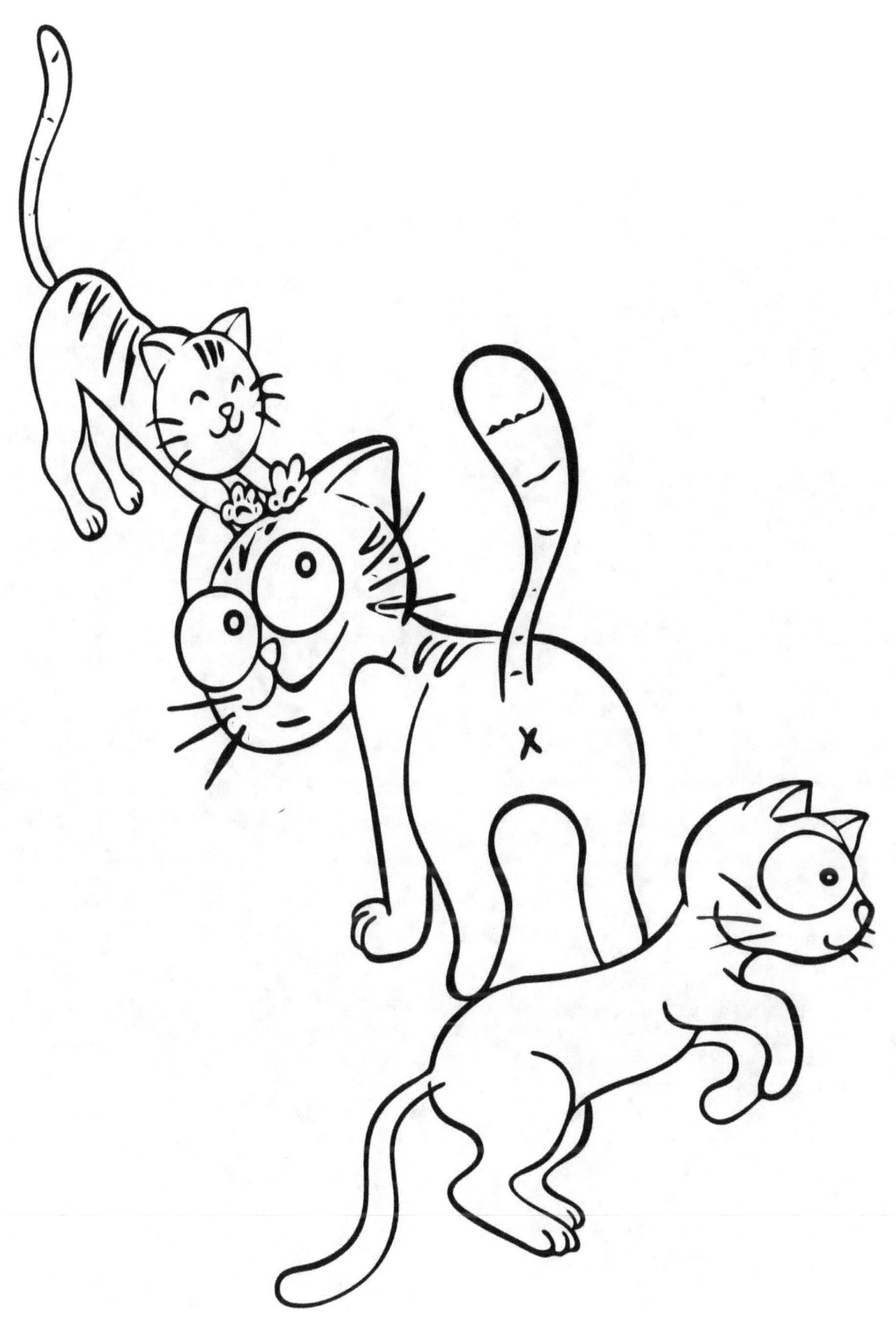

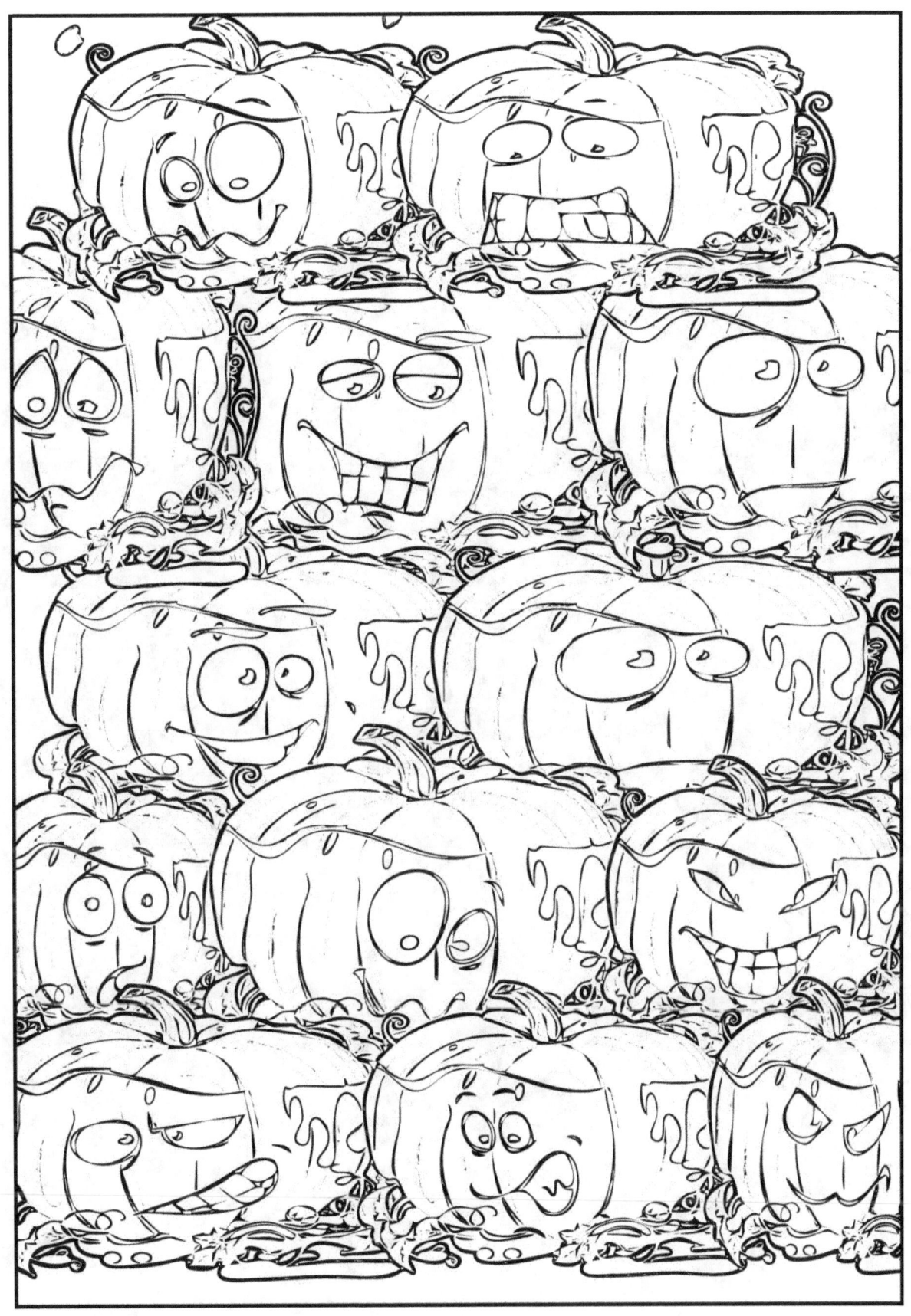

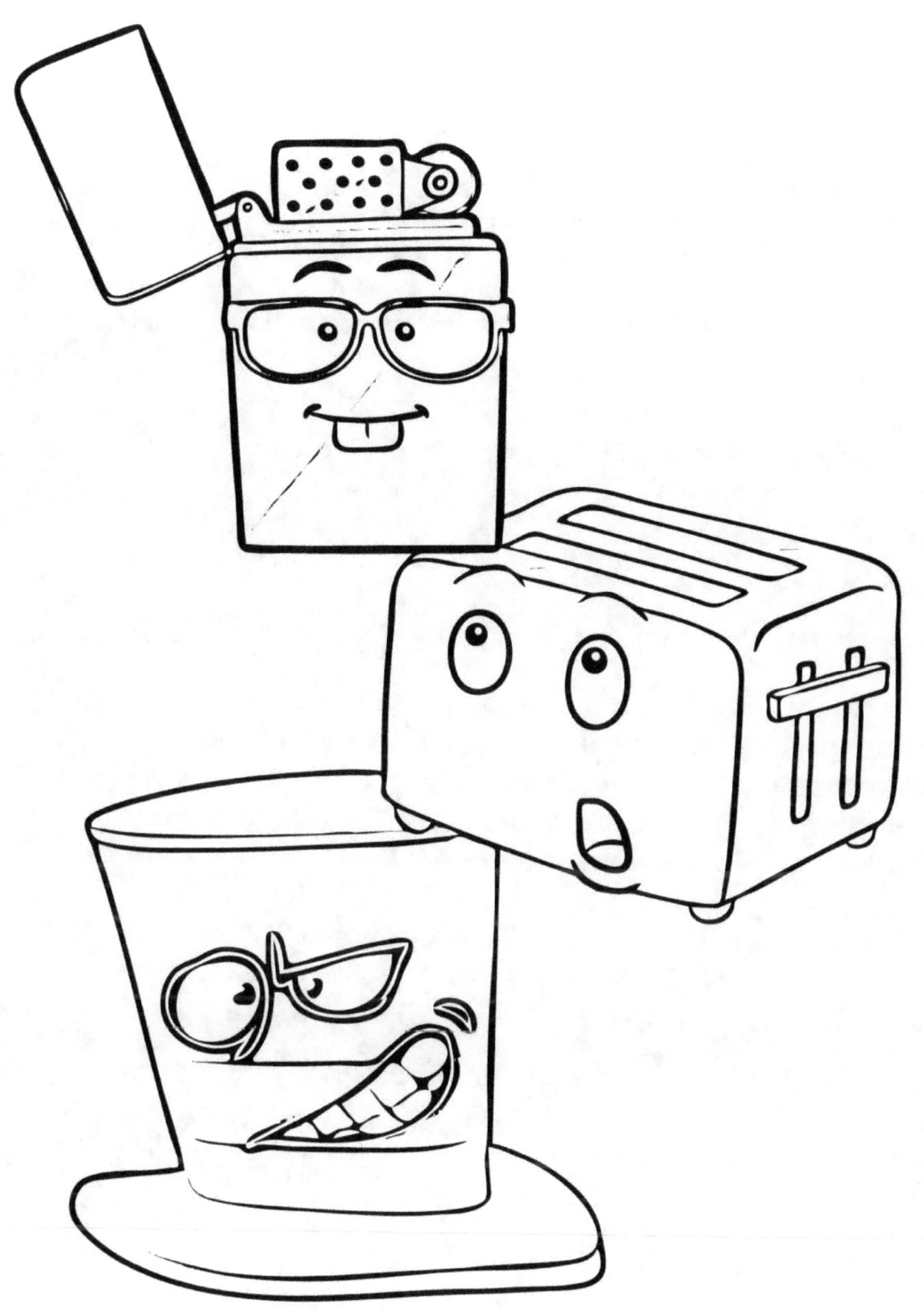

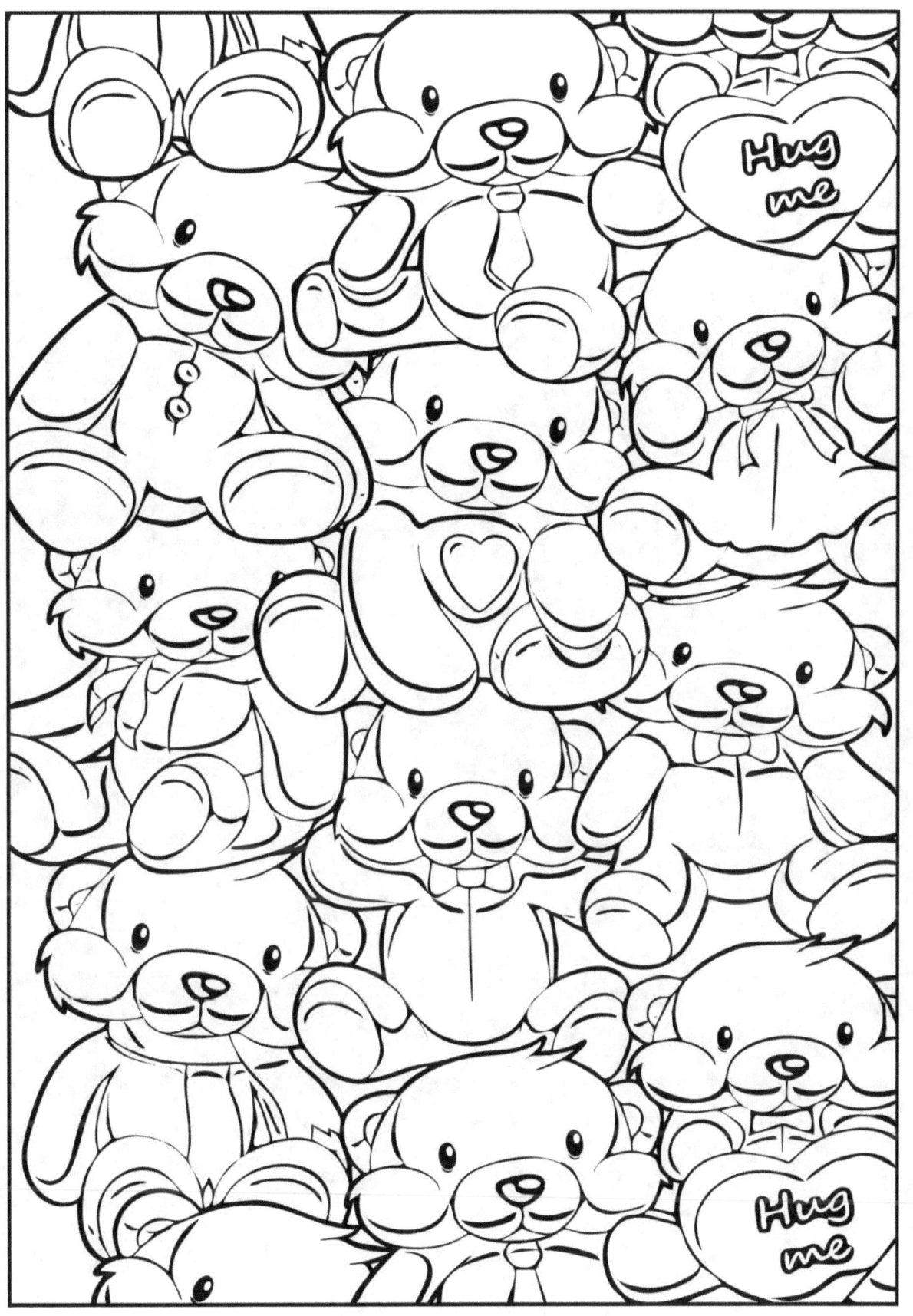

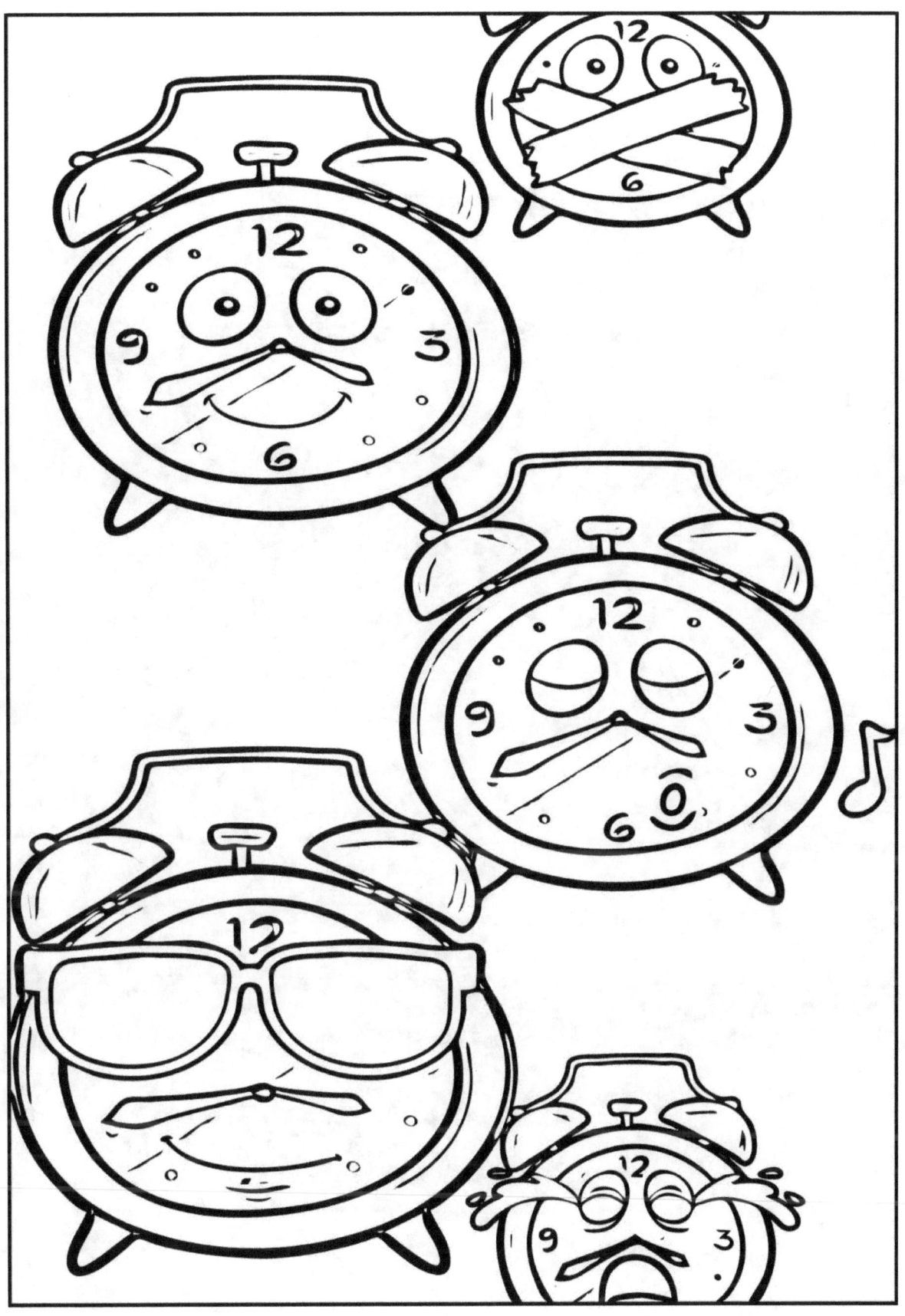

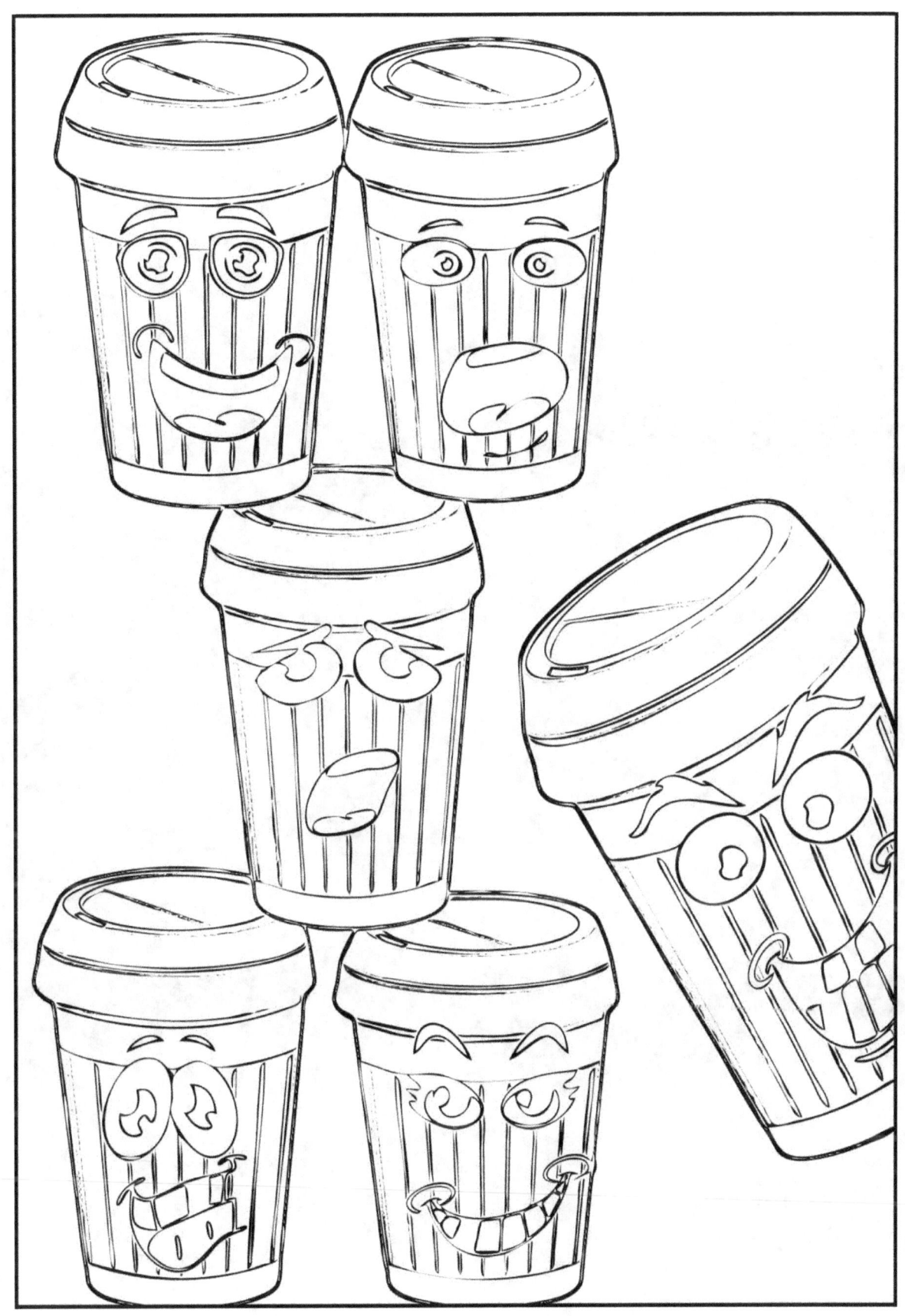

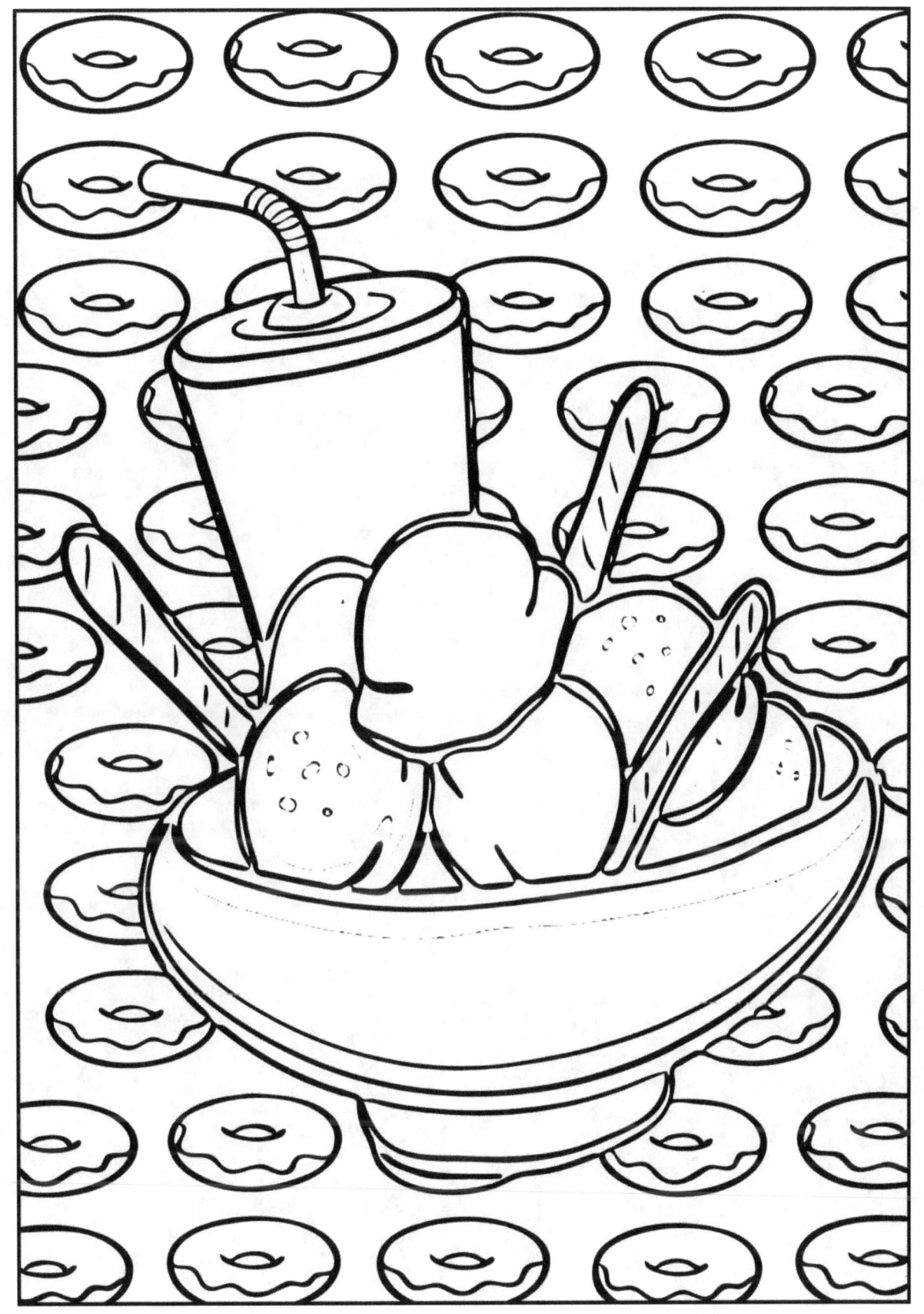

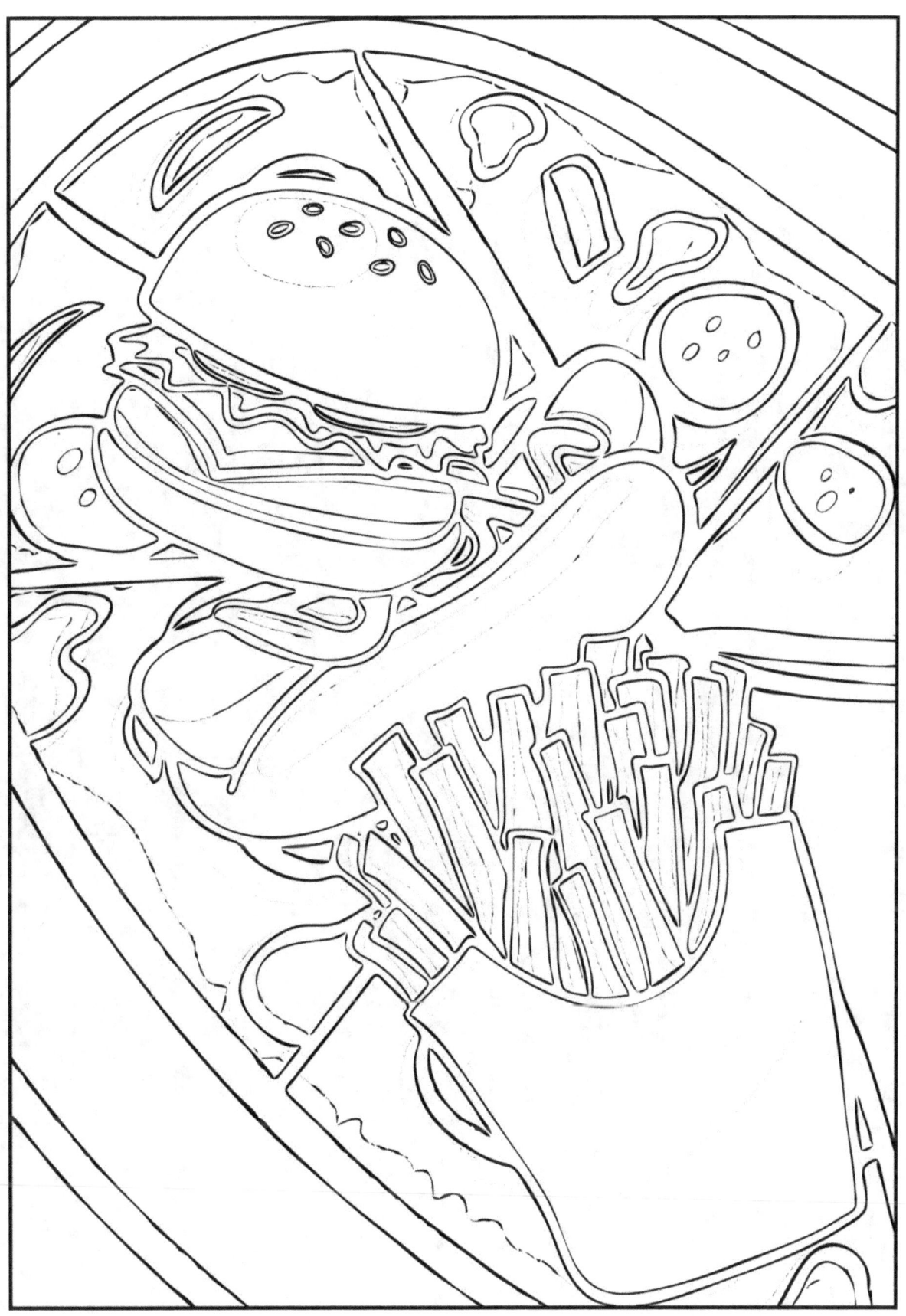

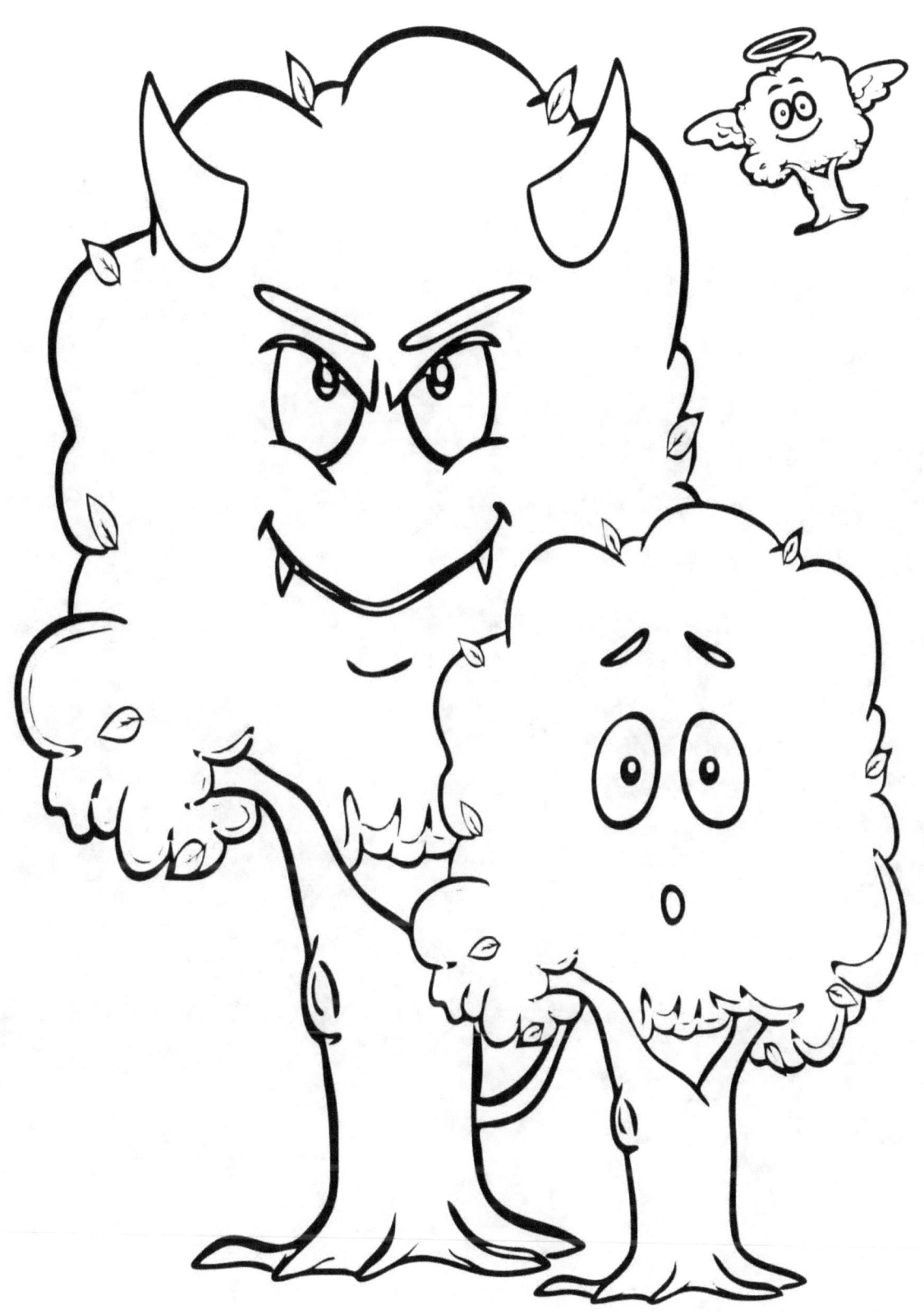

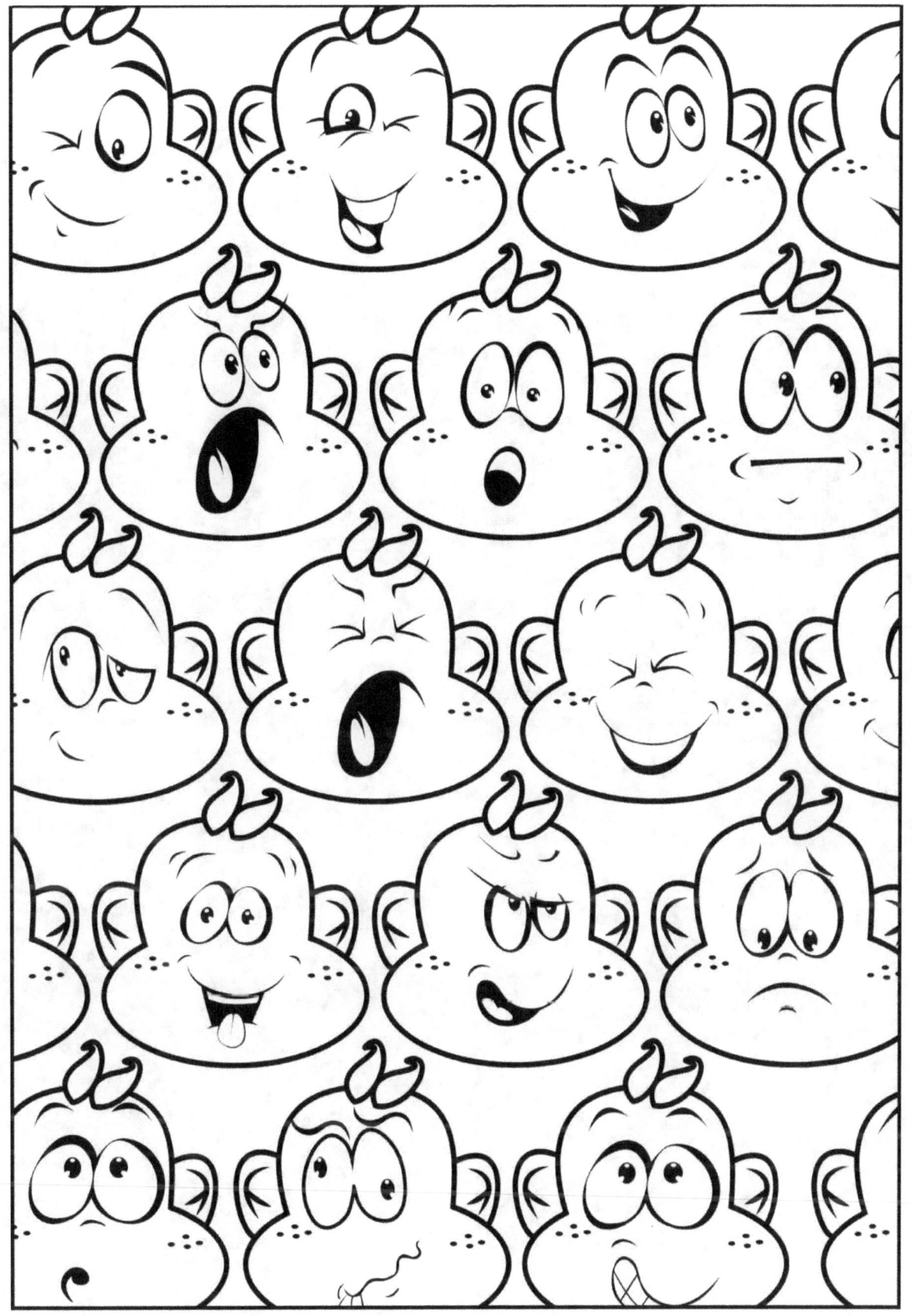

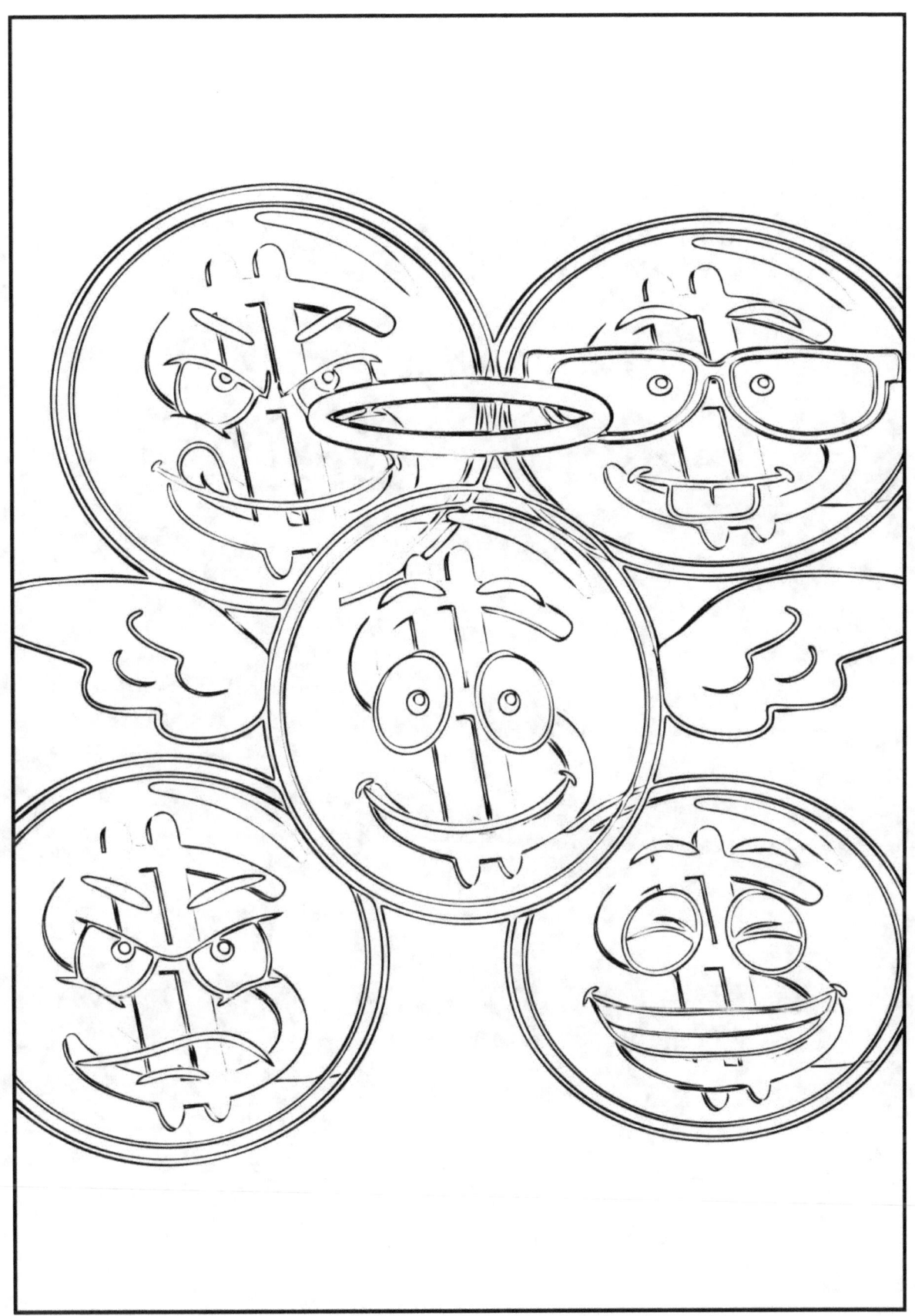

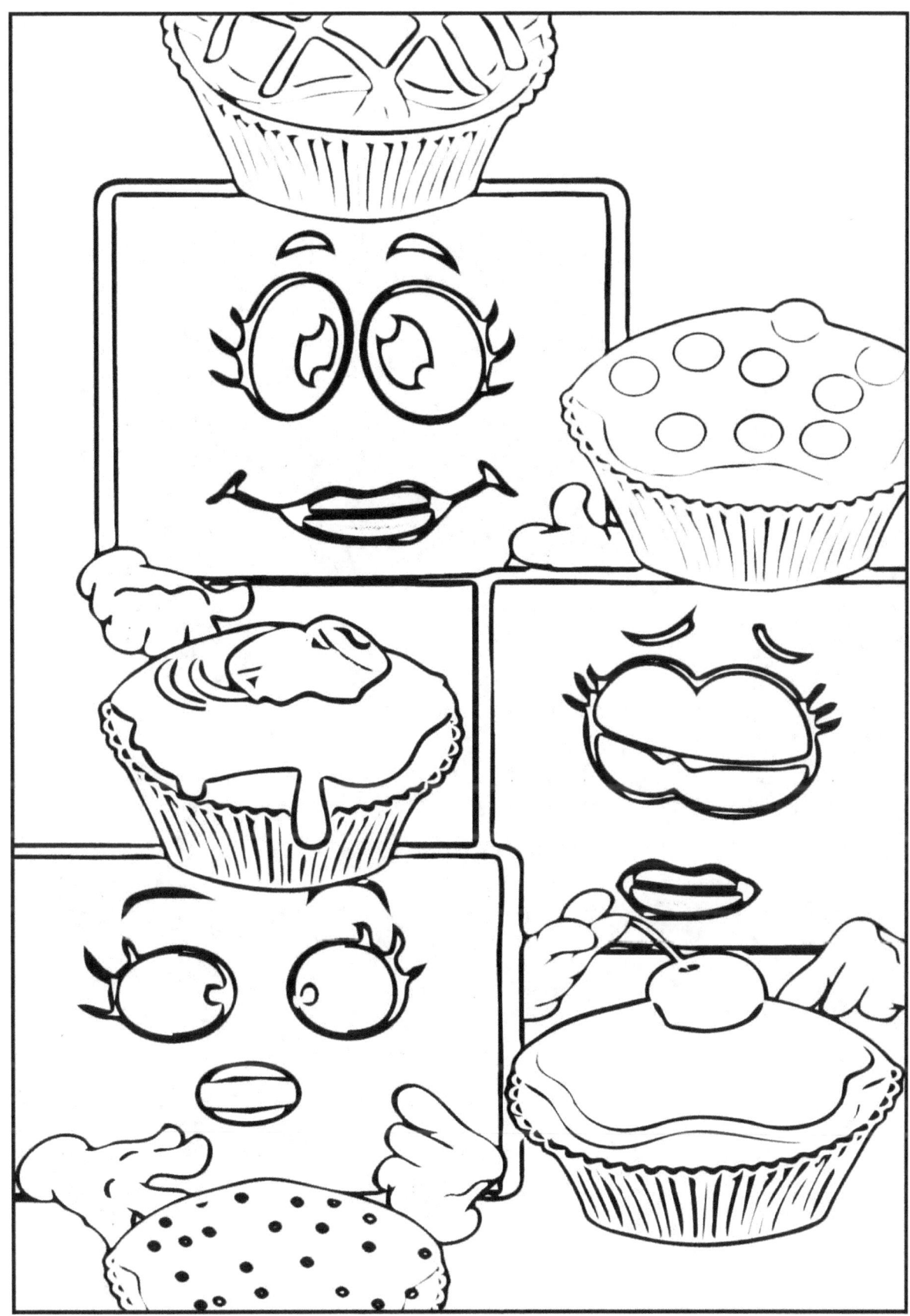

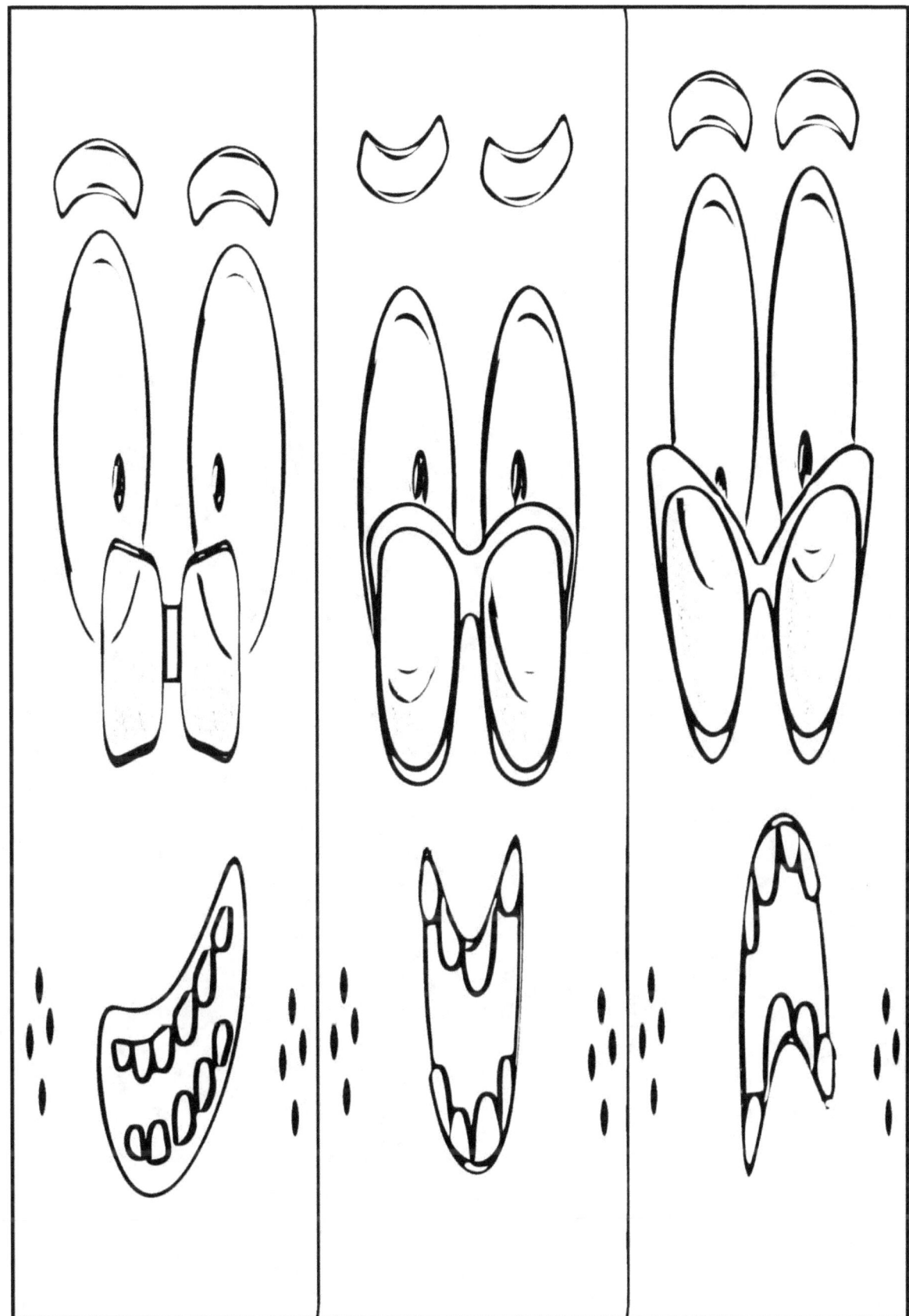

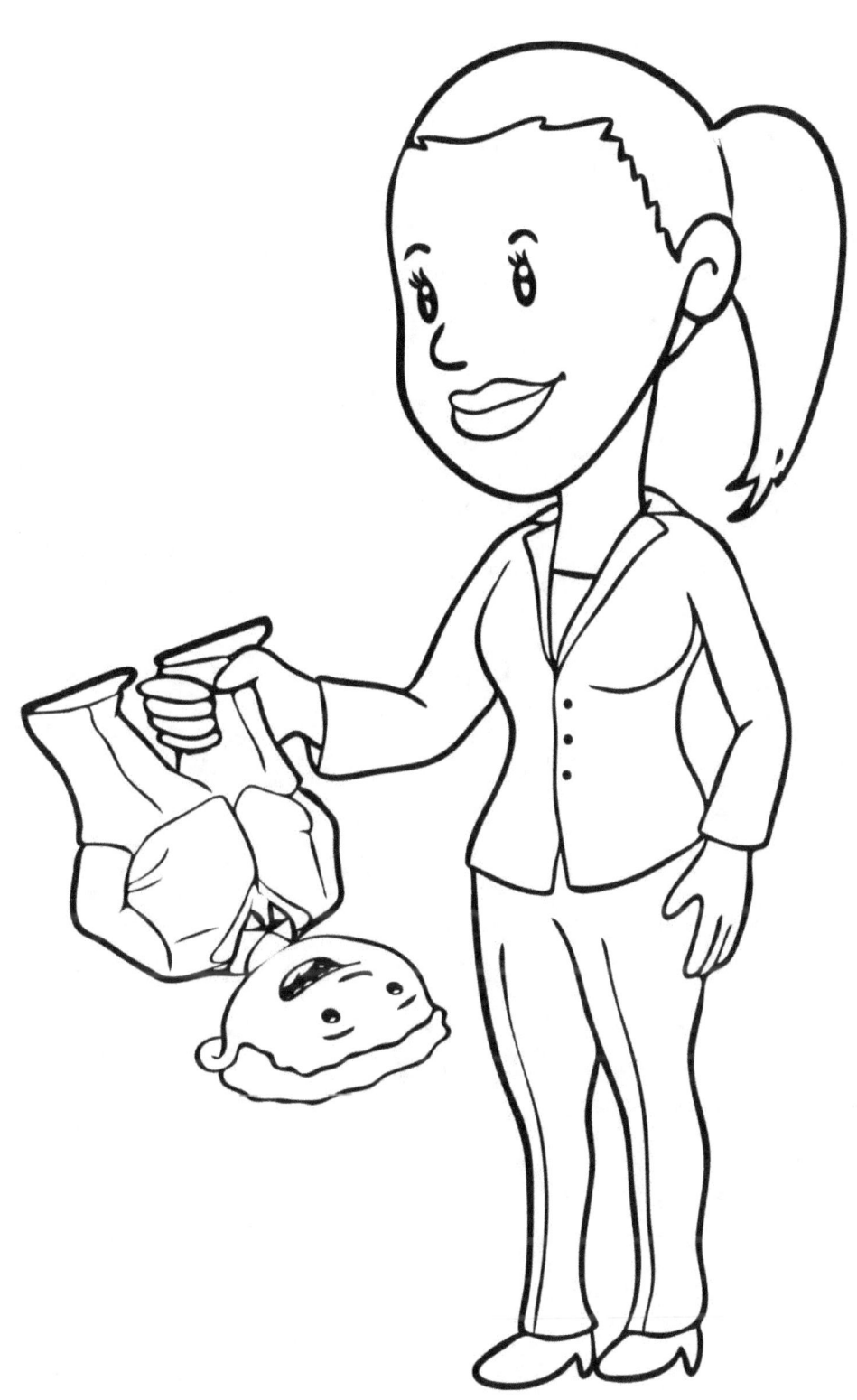

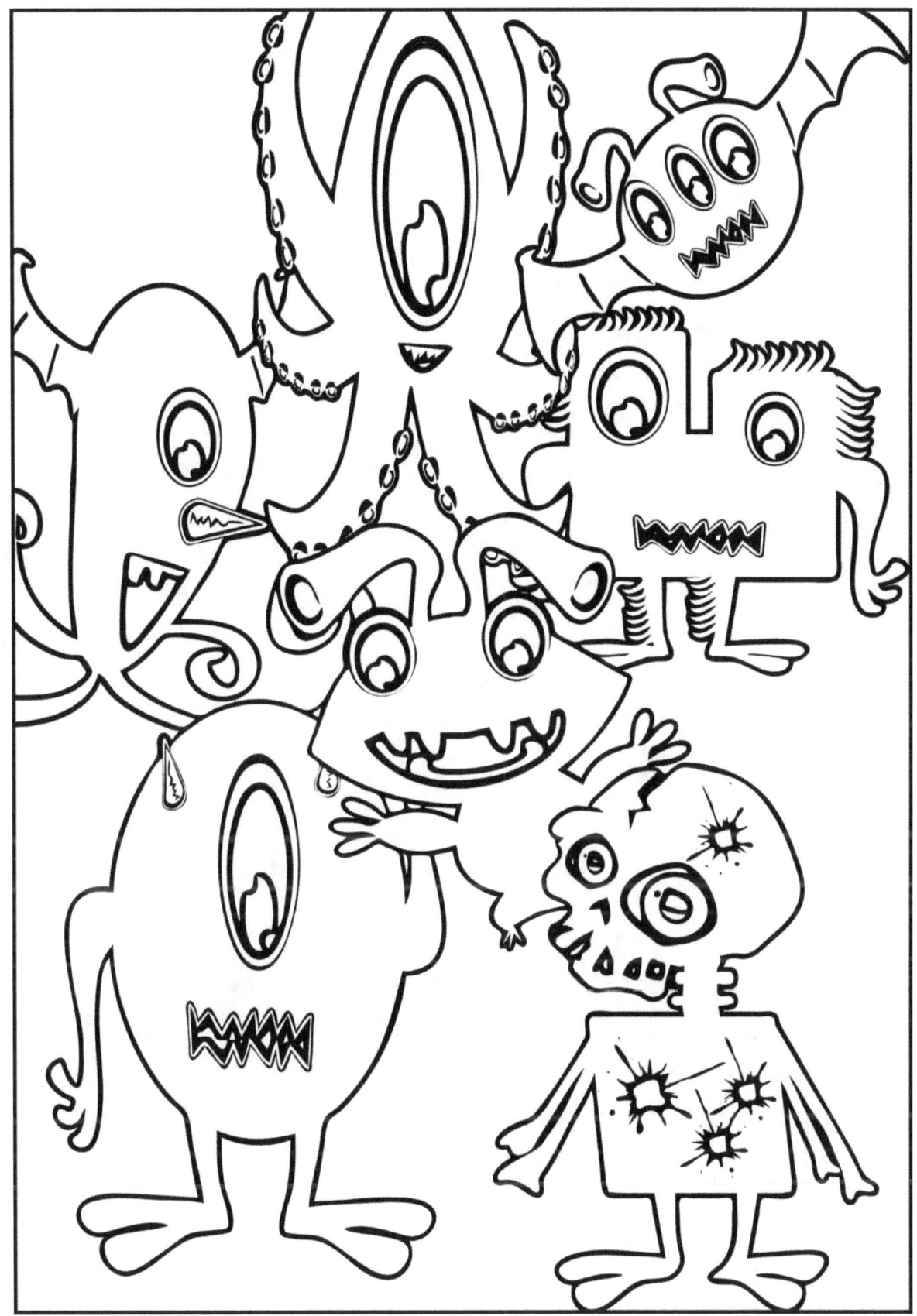

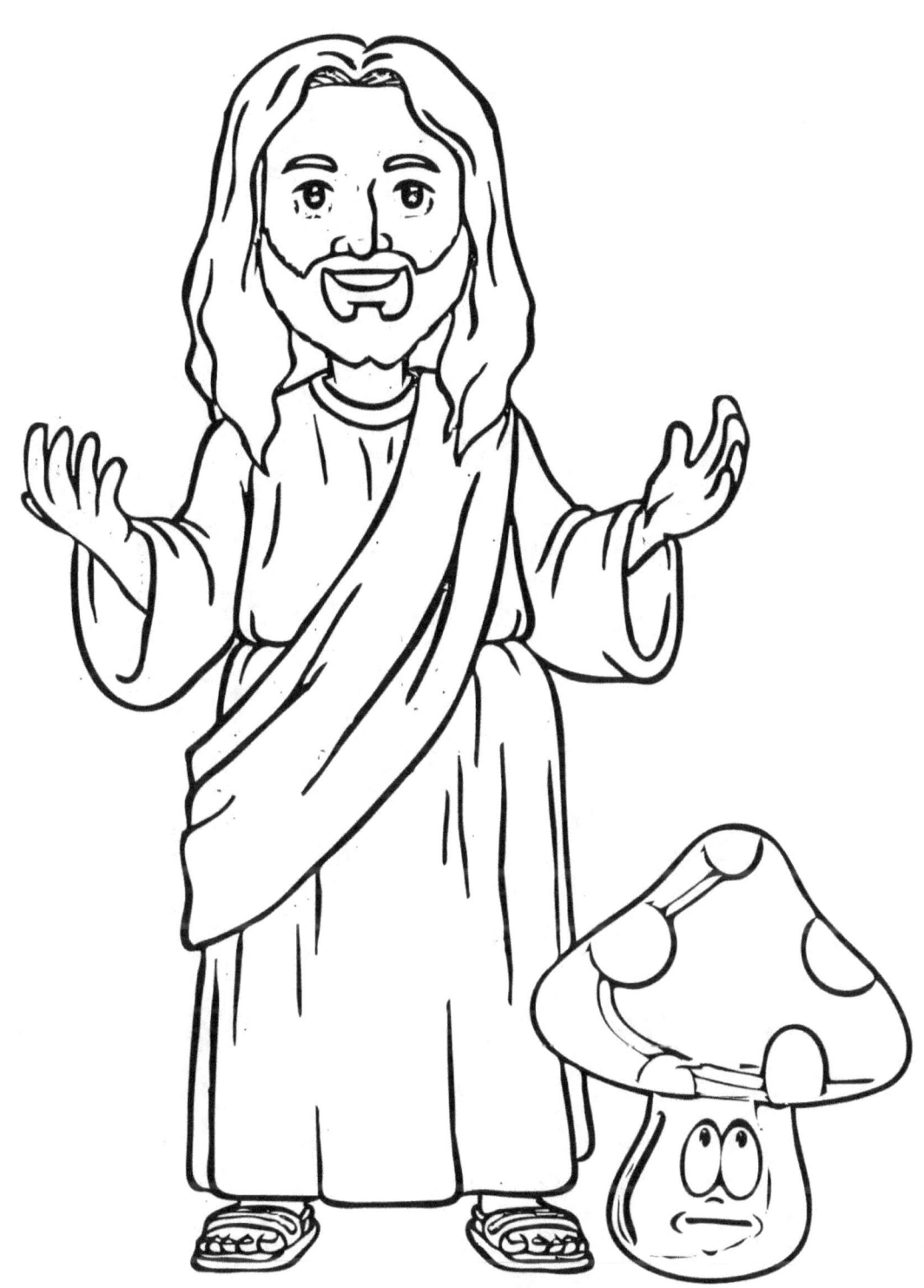

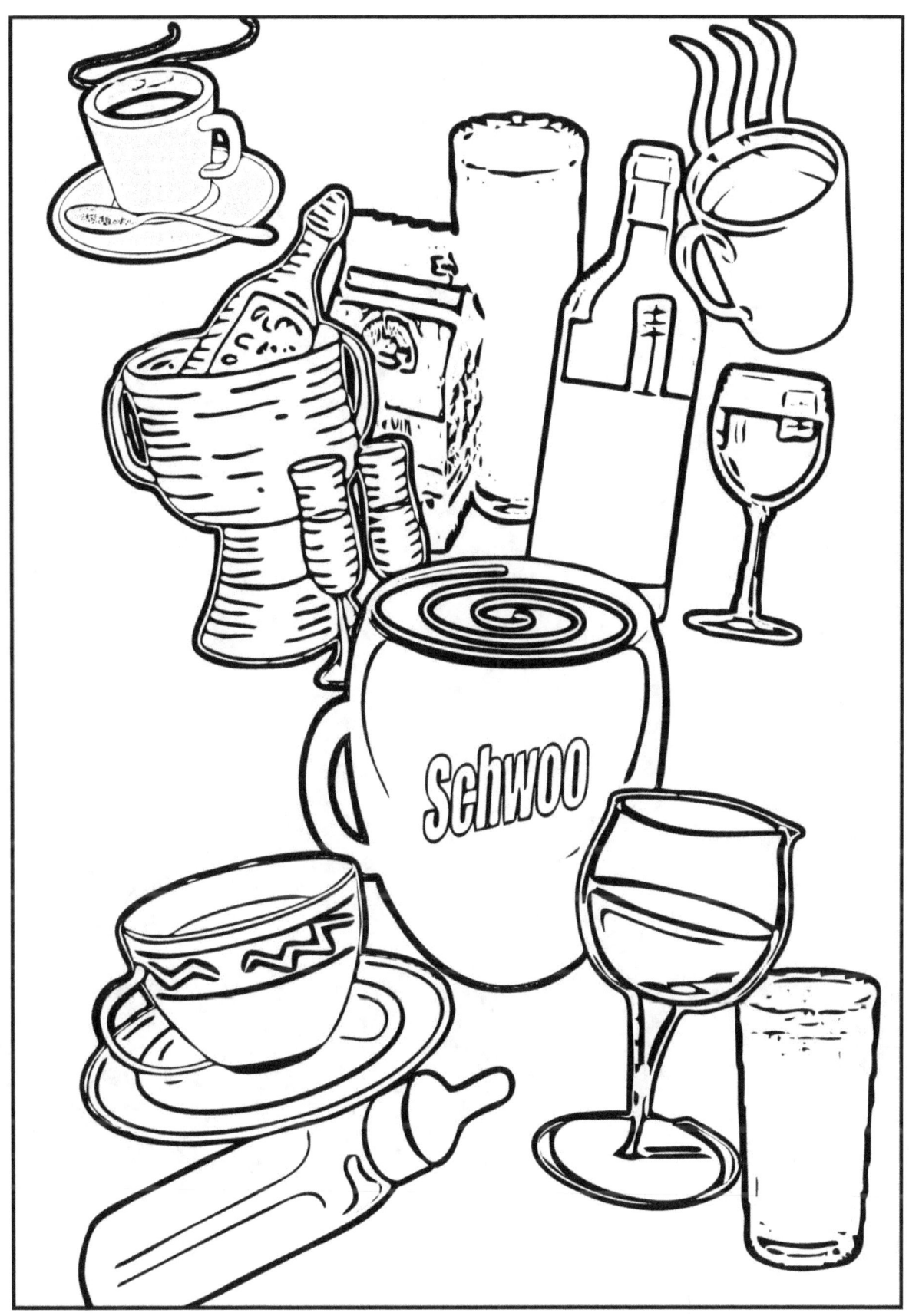

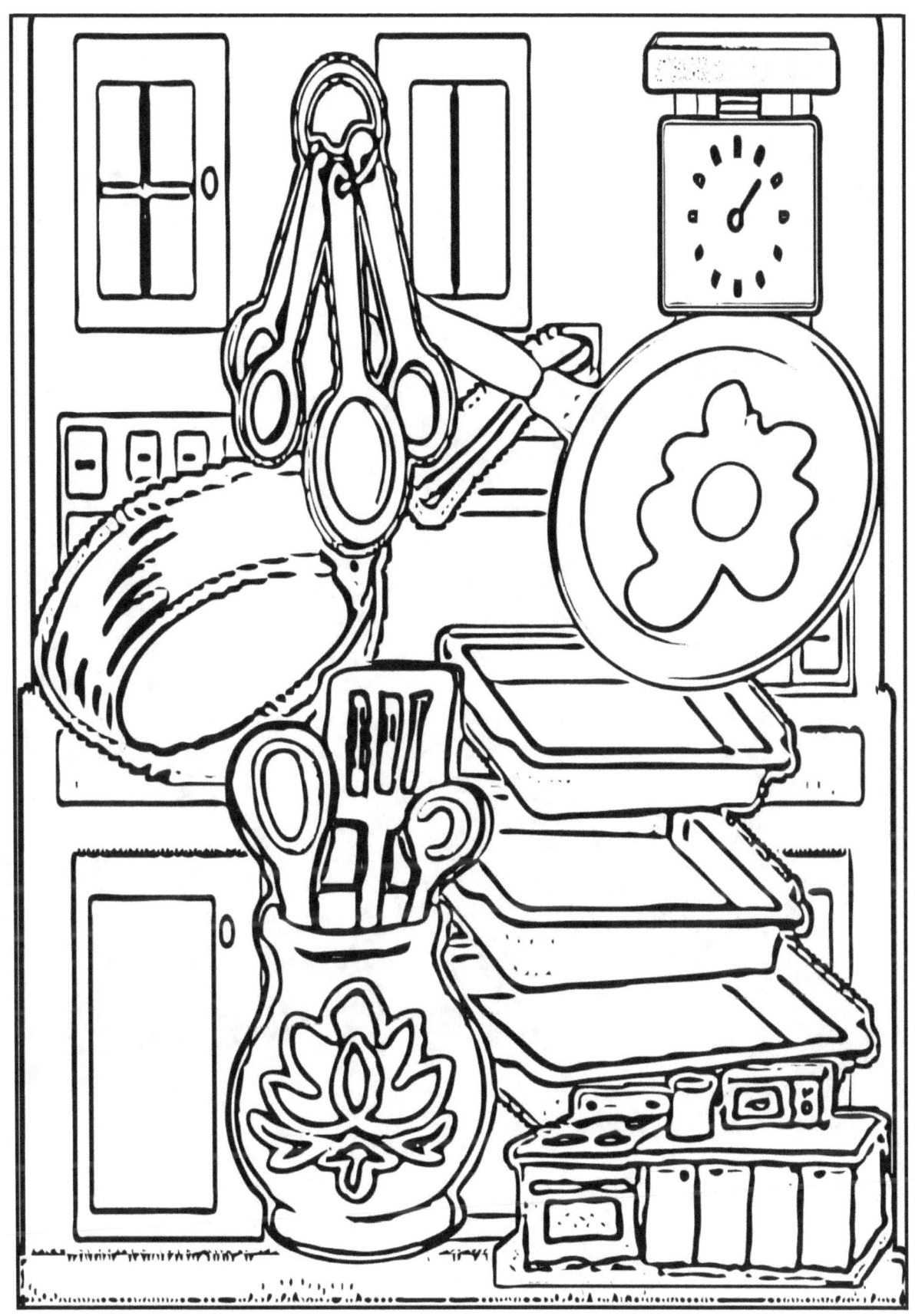

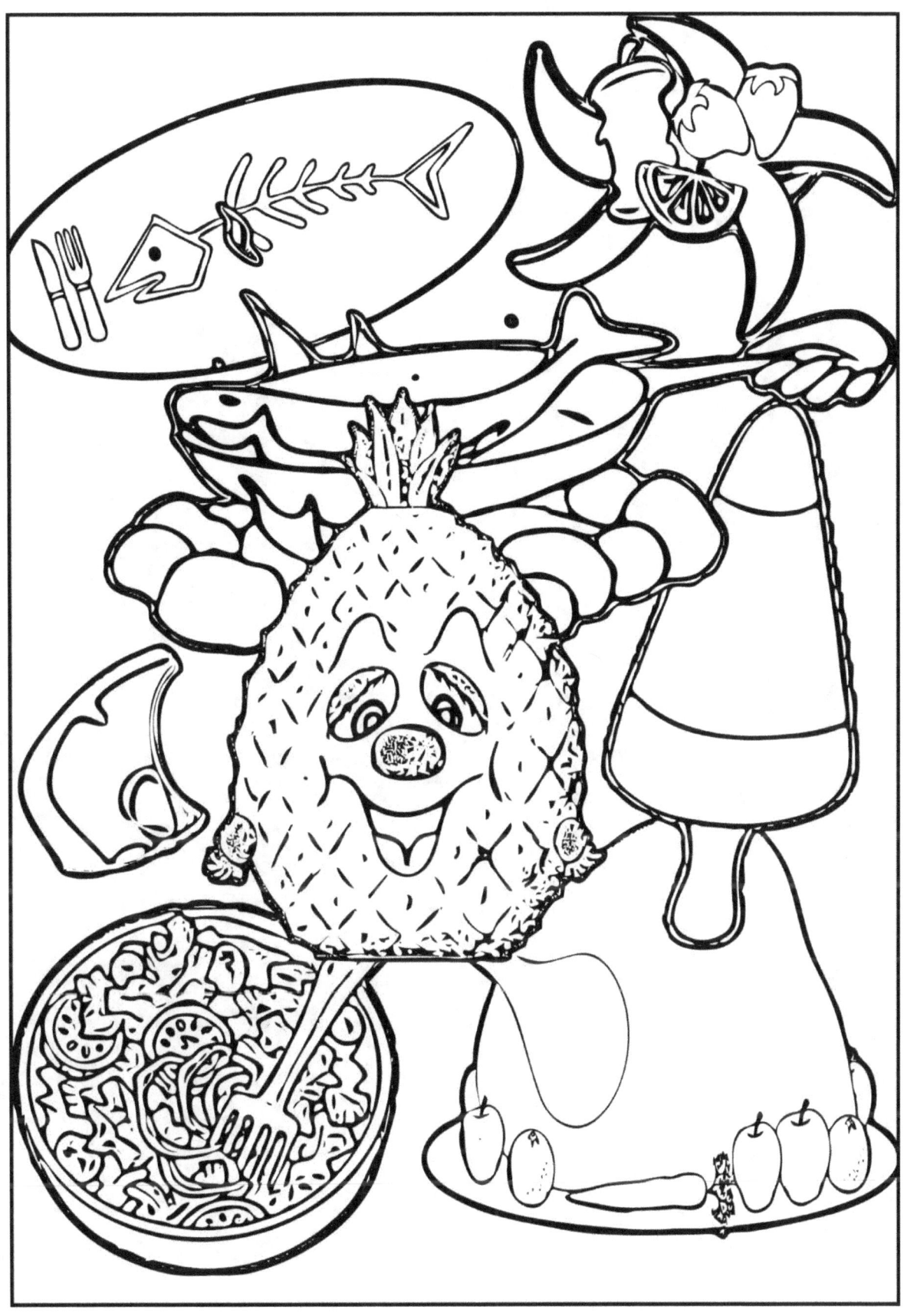

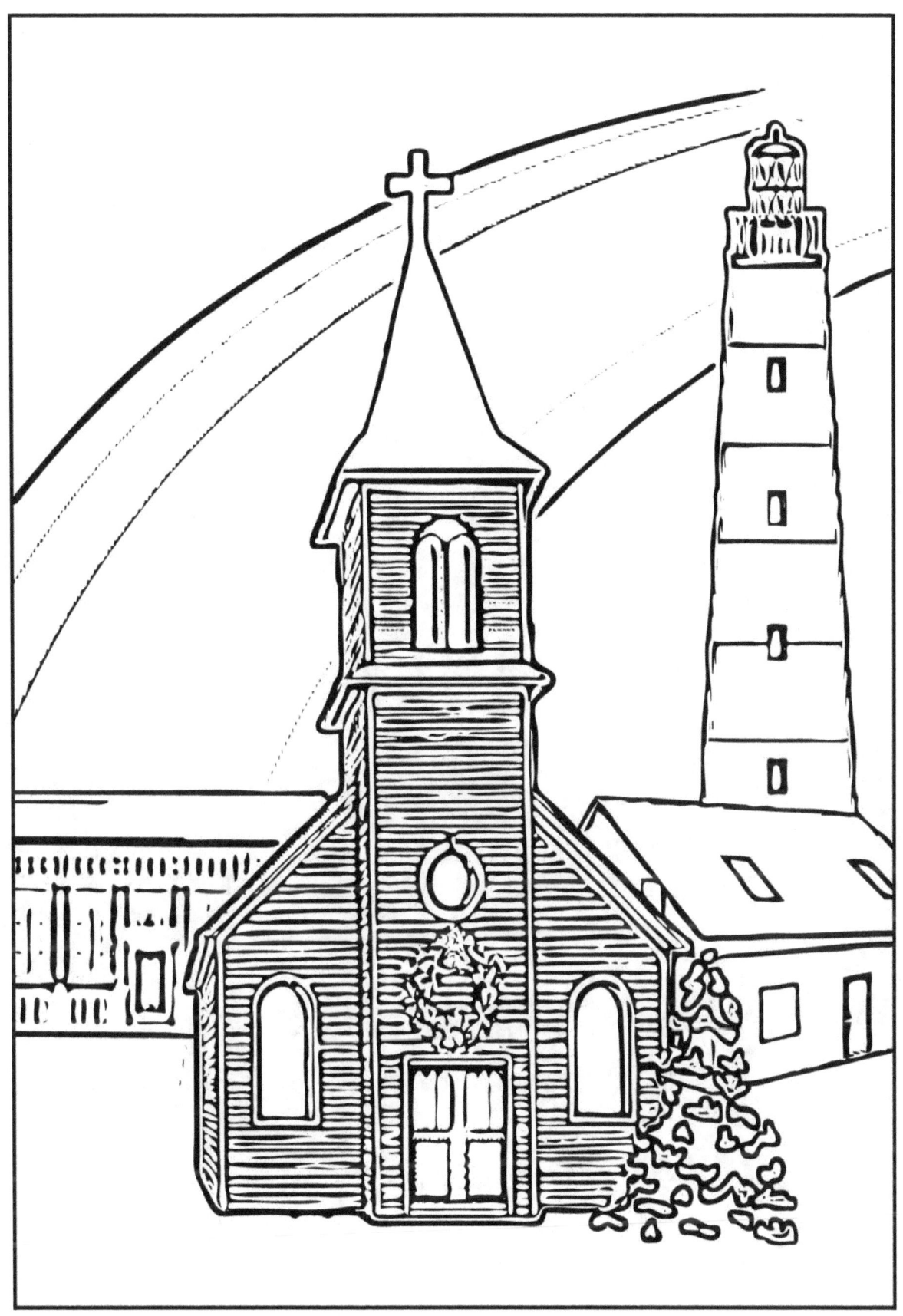

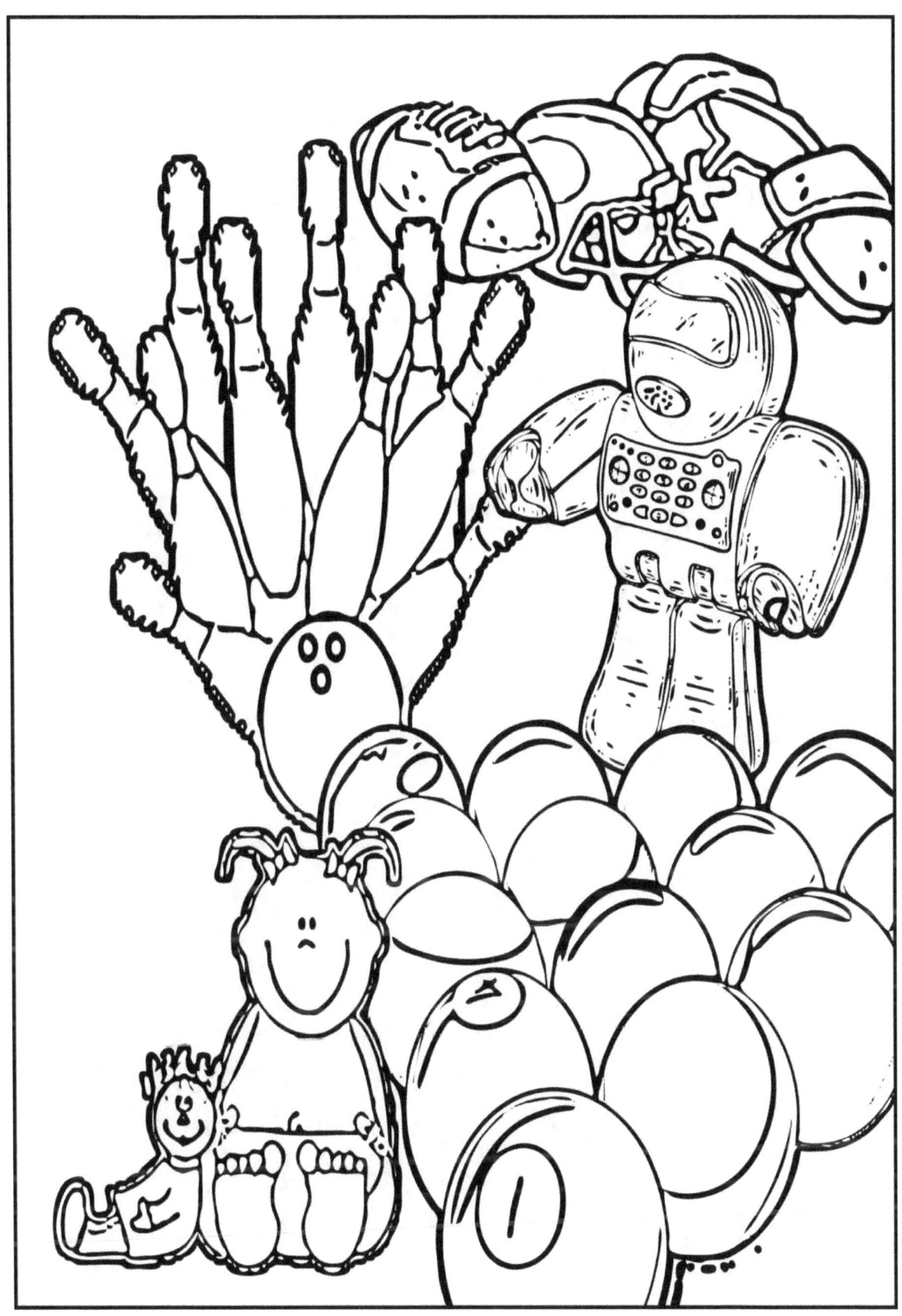

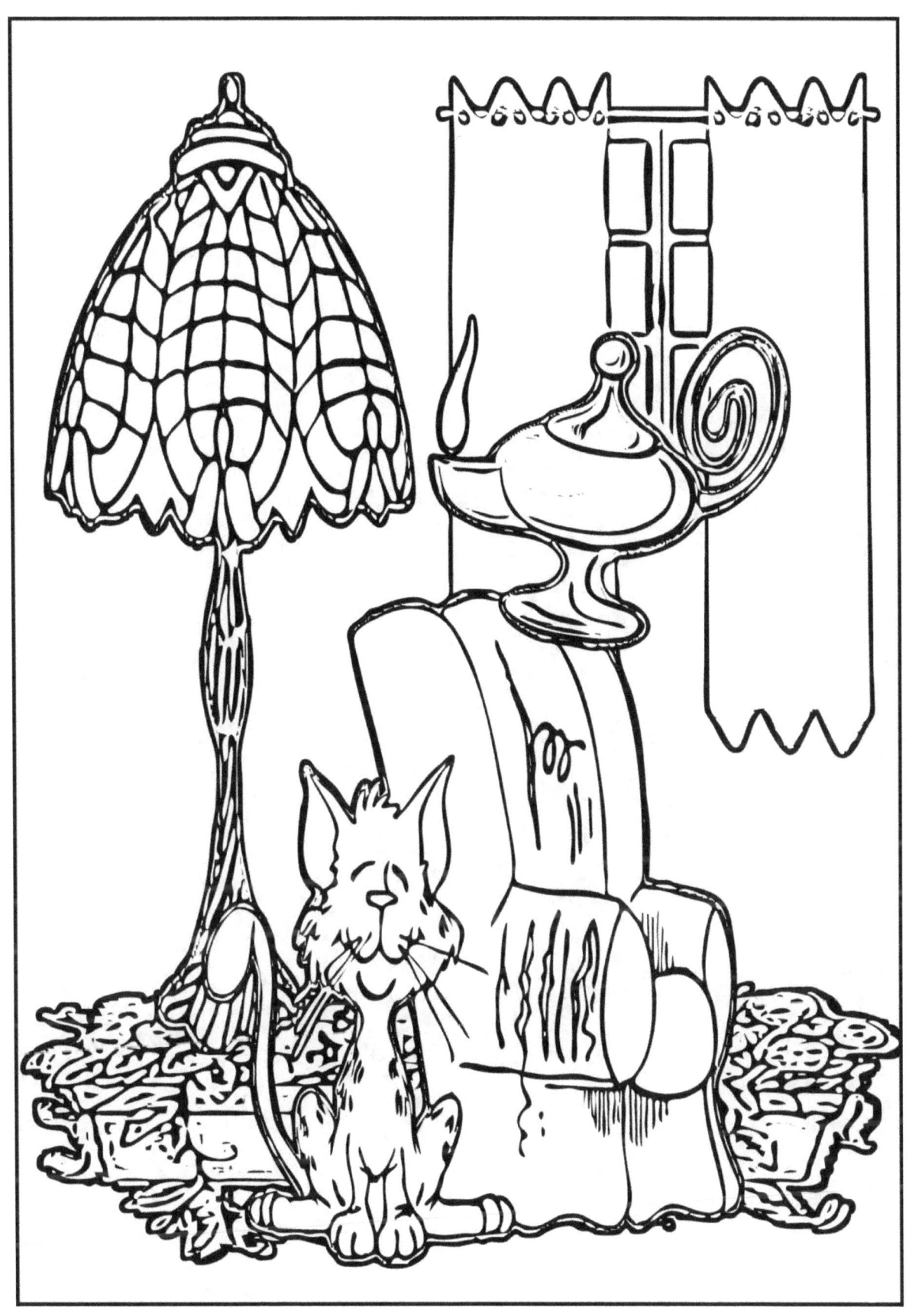

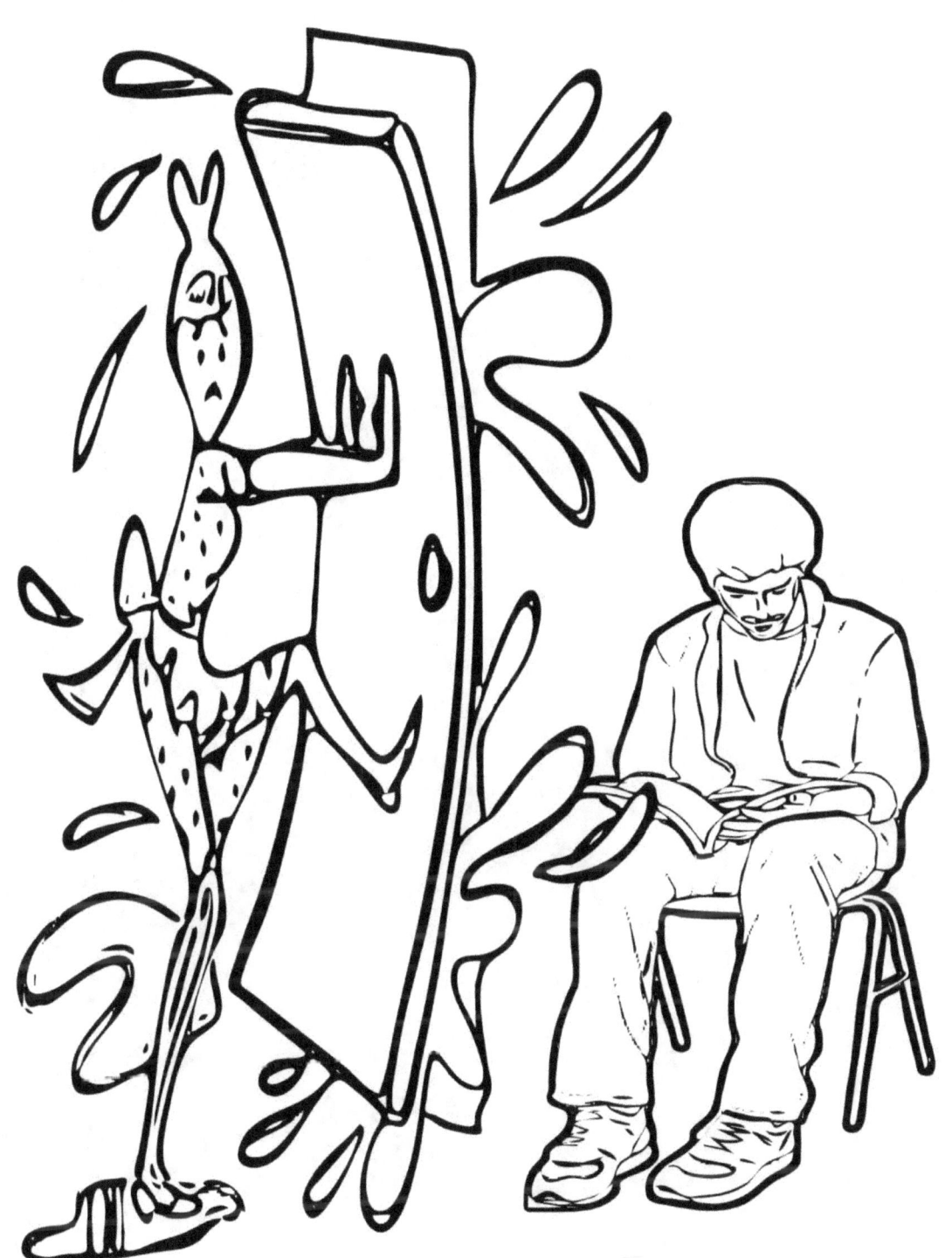

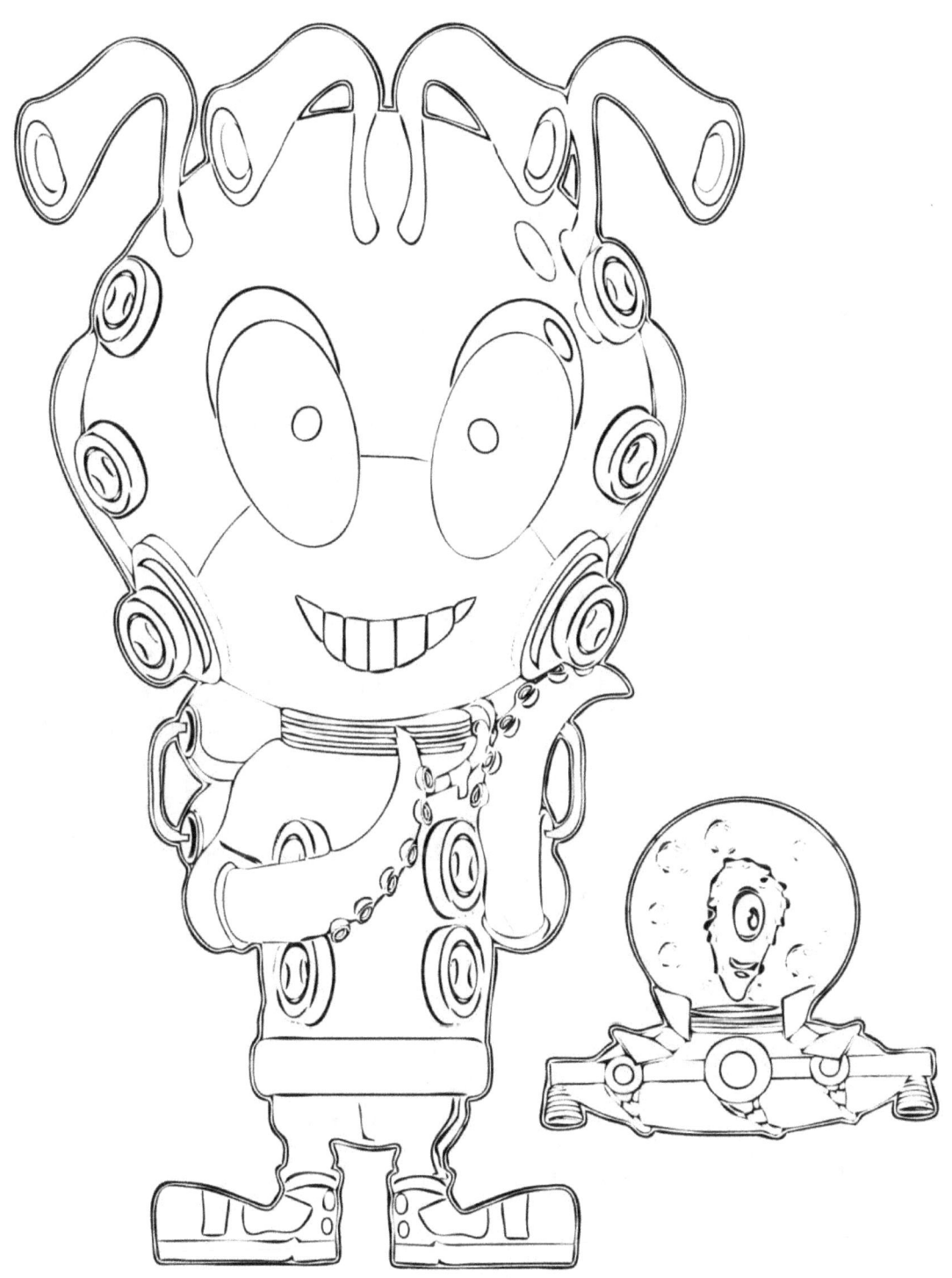

www.ingramcontent.com/pod-product-compliance
Lightning Source LLC
Chambersburg PA
CBHW081504170526
45166CB00008B/2555